FEED YOUR BEST FRIEND BETTER™

Easy, Nutritious Meals and Treats for Dogs

RICK WOODFORD

Photography by Alicia Dickerson Griffith

Andrews McMeel
Publishing, LLC

Kansas City · Sydney · London

Andrews McMeel Publishing, LLC
an Andrews McMeel Universal company
1130 Walnut Street, Kansas City, Missouri 64106

www.andrewsmcmeel.com

12 13 14 15 16 RR2 10 9 8 7 6 5 4 3 2 1

ISBN: 978-1-4494-0993-7

Library of Congress Control Number: 2011932641

Book design by Holly Ogden
Photography by Alicia Dickerson Griffith, www.fourleggedphoto.com

The information contained in this book is not intended to replace regular visits with a qualified veterinarian or to diagnose deficiencies or diseases in your pet. Before starting your pet on a special diet or supplementing your pet's food, always check with your veterinarian about your pet's specific needs. The information and recipes in this book are intended to benefit dogs as part of a healthy diet in conjunction with veterinary supervision, and while every effort was made to assure that the information and recipes are nutritionally sound and balanced for dogs, the author and publisher are not liable for any adverse effects your dog may experience while on these diets.

ATTENTION: SCHOOLS AND BUSINESSES
Andrews McMeel books are available at quantity discounts with bulk purchase for educational, business, or sales promotional use. For information, please e-mail the Andrews McMeel Publishing Special Sales Department: specialsales@amuniversal.com

FEED YOUR BEST FRIEND BETTER™

To Jackson, my best friend

There's a whining at the threshold,

There's a scratching at the floor,

To work! To work! In Heaven's name!

The wolf is at the door!

— C. P. S. GILMAN

CONTENTS

FOREWORD

For fifteen thousand years, dogs and humans have kindled a deep relationship like no other pairing on the planet. At the center of that relationship is food. Feeding our dogs every day is part of the unwritten, unspoken deal we've made in return for their protection, their aid in hunting and herding, and, for most of us nowadays, their companionship. We love to feed our dogs, and our dogs love to eat.

As we uphold our end of the bargain, we have many choices in what and how we feed our furry friends, just as we have choices for ourselves. Our lifestyles, budgets, health consciousness, and culinary ambitions all influence what we put into the food bowls and on our plates. What Rick Woodford has done with this book is to provide a carefully researched and kitchen-tested group of canine recipes and guidelines for people who love to cook.

For those who are pressed for time or worried about diving into a home-prepared diet headfirst, Rick helps us choose top-quality commercial diets to act as a nutritionally balanced foundation. Then the fun really begins. Ahead of you and your best friend are dozens of tasty, wholesome meals, each full of fresh and nutritious ingredients. Rick goes beyond merely inventing yummy meals for our dogs. He understands the responsibility we take on when we choose the ingredients that go into our pets' food, and provides guidance to avoid some of the pitfalls that can accompany feeding an unbalanced homemade food for a prolonged time.

As a holistic veterinarian, I have witnessed firsthand the healing power of food, whether commercial or homemade, that has been prepared in a mindful, loving way. It's important to seek the advice of your veterinarian if your dog does not seem to be thriving on the food you're preparing; if your dog seems to be doing great, yearly exams and blood work are still important, especially if feeding any home-prepared food regularly.

Feeding your dog should be a joyful experience for both you and your dog. With the help of the following pages, you can nurture not only the chef within and the health of your dog but also the bond between you and your best friend. Enjoy!

Nancy Curran
Doctor of Veterinary Medicine
Two Rivers Veterinary Clinic, PC

INTRODUCTION: MY BEST FRIEND, JACKSON

Jackson and I had shared an apartment for three months by the time our first April 14 rolled around. When I opened the door, we both ran to one another, happy to be reunited after an eight-hour shift at work; mine building databases and analyzing data, Jackson's loudly guarding the house from the comfort of my bed. When being interviewed by Jackson's former owners, I was surprised to learn that his birthday was the same as mine: April 14. On our first birthday together, a package arrived from my mom, and our birthday gifts were inside. Holding the box, I let Jackson tear off the brown paper wrapping, and then I examined the contents: a toy for Jackson to tear apart, and a dog food cookbook for me. The book was entertaining, and it seemed like a nice idea to cook for your dog, but it was soon moved to a bookshelf and never opened again. After all, dogs eat dog food, right?

At five years old, Jackson was still a terror on walks and mischievous when unsupervised. One of his parents had been a Belgian Malanoise, and that part of his heritage made Jackson a fierce protector and intelligent student. The other parent must have been a Labrador Retriever; inside the house Jackson was playful and loving. His genetic mélange somehow left Jackson with ears that were ridiculously small for his shrunken apple head that was also too small for his body. Still, he was adorable, and his playful antics charmed everyone who met him.

I had wanted a dog because my life as a bachelor left me feeling lonely, and continually opening the door to an empty house was repetitively disappointing. The moment Jackson arrived, life changed. We raced one another to a nearby lagoon before work and took long walks around the neighborhood after dinner. I would hide and Jackson would try to find me, or I'd hide a toy for a game of "Find It!" When we weren't playing tug-of-war with the empty hide of a stuffed animal, school was in session and Jackson learned to turn on a lamp, close doors, and retrieve items for me. I took Jackson everywhere, and hundreds of miles under tennis shoes and paws transformed our relationship from being just roommates to being best friends.

Three years into our friendship, I noticed a small bump on Jackson's neck. "Probably another bee sting," I told myself. A couple of weeks later, the bump was a bit larger. A series of appointments and tests earned us a referral to an oncologist. We began turning back to the house after walking only a few blocks, and our runs stopped altogether. Jackson's appetite disappeared and he spent days lying in his bed, not wanting to be bothered with food or walks. It seemed as though he had three paws in the grave and I was desperately holding onto the fourth.

Just a few days before Christmas, Dr. Freeman, our veterinary oncologist, called to deliver the verdict while I was grocery shopping. "Jackson has lymphoma, and will probably live for another nine to twelve months if he responds well to treatment." Cell phone reception was spotty at the grocery store, so I stood across from the meat counter, afraid to lose the connection. That night I went through the checkout with two steaks on the conveyor belt and tears in my eyes. It was Jackson's first meal from the stovetop, and each bite was delivered by hand.

One skipped meal raised my concern, but a series of days without food meant Jackson was not receiving any nutrition to help in his battle. To encourage his appetite, I started throwing turkey and vegetables into a pot. Jackson ate heartily, then returned to his bed in the corner. I fed him homemade meals off and on, noting that he eagerly ate what I cooked and often refused food on the days when it was just dry kibble. As Jackson's interest in food picked up, and his eagerness for walks was restored, I began increasing the amount of homemade food I was giving him and decreasing his dry food. With a new sense of vigor, Jackson began chasing our puppy, Raleigh, around the backyard, his activity a stark contrast to the diagnosis we had been given.

Seeing the difference in Jackson made me feel that I could help other dogs as well. I quit my job to read every veterinary manual and recipe book I could find, while analyzing the nutrition in hundreds of recipes. After six months I opened Dog Stew so that all dogs could benefit from real nutrition. My logo was Jackson sitting at his bowl, licking his chops. Concerned pup-parents started asking me to help dogs with skin problems, kidney disease, heart disease, diabetes, cancer, and liver issues. I never said no, but I never said yes until I fully researched the nutritional requirements of each ailment. Each dog ate happily and his or her condition improved. Assisted by my mother, I cooked and delivered thousands of meals every month, and my customers started calling me "The Dog Food Dude."

Meetings with veterinarians to introduce my service left them cautiously interested. Understanding their hesitation, I asked that they suggest my services as a trial when all other options had been exhausted. A few weeks later, I received a call from Wilma's owners. Wilma was a lovely Dalmatian with kidney disease, and was on a prolonged hunger strike. I made up a batch of food and headed over for my first delivery. Wilma's owner was beside himself with worry. I asked whether Wilma had eaten that morning, and he returned a glance that indicated it was a silly question: "She never eats." I showed him how to portion the food and warm it with a little water, and suddenly he stopped me. "Don't feel bad if she doesn't eat your food." We set the food bowl down, and Wilma gave the food an investigative sniff, looked up once at us, and dove into the bowl. She didn't look up again until the bowl was empty, and quadruple-checked that she hadn't missed anything. Suddenly her owner grabbed me and gave me a big hug. "Thank you, thank you, thank you," he repeated over and over. With Wilma and many other dogs, I was finding that even though the food was meant for the dogs, it meant a great deal more to the people who loved their pets.

Eighteen months after Jackson was diagnosed with lymphoma, he showed no signs of slowing down. At a checkup Dr. Freeman delivered her final verdict: "I rarely get to tell people this, but you don't need to bring Jackson back. He's in remission." We owed the chemotherapy regimen for arresting the growth of Jackson's cancer but gave credit to real food for his renewed vigor and a reason to keep on fighting. Instead of wasting away, Jackson was once again a vibrant, happy dog.

Unfortunately the recession hit and my funding ran out. Customers begged me to continue and actually offered to pay more for the service. One customer bought one of my freezers with the stipulation that I stock it with four months of food for her two dogs. My dream started to take a different shape when I realized my research and experience could be used to write this book.

I spent many days in the kitchen testing recipes, and Jackson, Raleigh, and I continued bonding over thousands of meals, cookies, and walks. Jackson even took up running again. When I met the love of my life, we welcomed three more additions to our pack: Duncan, Baxter, and Chloe. The house thundered under the footsteps of our "herd of puppalo," and the bed became really crowded. Jackson practically pranced as he led his pack along walks. We eventually wore Jackson's body out simply from old age. Rather than letting him succumb to cancer, good meals and plenty of love allowed him to live three years beyond his last visit with the oncologist. I'm extremely grateful that the time spent in the kitchen allowed me so many extra years with my best friend. It makes me wish I had started cooking for him when I received that first cookbook.

Let me show you how you can provide simple, practical nutrition based upon real foods. I'm an information junkie; I'll do the heavy lifting of the data. You only need to pick a spoon. While you're preparing dinner, maybe there are a few antioxidant gold mines you could share with your dog rather than throwing them out. Share the right foods with your dog, so that he too can have a happy, healthy, and long life. If Grandma has a dog she loves, get the grandkids to make her some Christmas cookies for the dog. They'll both appreciate a Gingerbread Mailman Cookie (page 88) each time the cookie jar is opened. When it's your dog's birthday, set an example for your children. Emphasize simple nutrition over sugar-laden treats with a pot of homemade stew that you set in the slow cooker before you leave for work. It's a week's worth of meals for your dog, and you'll be surprised that it doesn't have to be done every day. Heck, most things you can cook alongside your own dinner once a month. Mix half and half with a good-quality dry food if it's what works best for you.

Have a little more time and want to use natural sources of nutrition for every member of your family at every meal? Supplement Stew (page 14) combined with most of the recipes in this book provides your four-legged kids nutrition beyond the complete and balanced formula; fresh foods full of antioxidants can help us all grow into active, healthy adults. Because our dogs grow older a little faster than we do, they sometimes need a little love and a specific meal for what ails them. Talk to your veterinarian about serving a Warm-Nose Meal instead of foods that are composed mostly of corn.

If you need a nutritional analysis of any recipe in this book, go to www.dogfooddude.com. I'll provide an analysis based upon the USDA's nutritional data and the National Research Council's recommendations—free of charge. Let's feed our best friends the same way many of us feed ourselves—fresh and local when we can, combined with foods that are still convenient and definitely not considered junk food. Whether it's a slice of apple, an egg, kale, or a smidgen of cheese, each food brings a unique flavor and nutritional profile to a meal. Start with teaspoons and tablespoons and you'll see that the nutrition in real foods is something that makes everybody's tail wag.

BEST FRIENDS DESERVE BETTER

In the 15,000 years since dog first introduced himself to man, countless dogs have hunted with us, protected our families, entertained us with their foolish antics, aided those who are handicapped, and provided company to the lonely. We in turn give them a warm place to sleep and a share of our larder. Food and love are the currency in our contract with dogs.

We squeeze onto a small portion of the couch to watch television with our canine best friends, and we let them hog the bed. We buy toys for them to tear apart and treats to keep them motivated. Our dogs protect our families and homes and never fail to greet us with a cheerful bark and an enthusiastically wagging tail. We shower them with love and affection, regardless of how much pet hair we're covered in as we leave the house. Yet the one thing that we often withhold and that will do the greatest good is real food.

Our culture is beginning to value how more sustainable foods and quality ingredients can enhance our well-being. Increasingly people are trading in the convenience of manufactured foods for simple meals prepared with fresh ingredients that not only taste better but also provide better nutrition. Meanwhile, our dogs watch us with envy, waiting for something more interesting than dry food, which is little more than fast food laced with a multivitamin. It's time we stopped coveting everything in the cupboard and refrigerator as "people food." Lasagne, with its onions, salt, pepper, and abundance of cheese, should certainly be reserved for the table as people food. However, pasta, fresh meat, herbs, and even a bit of cheese are simply foods—foods that can be shared with our best friends in moderate amounts.

THERE'S MORE IN FOOD THAN YOU KNOW

Secondary metabolites are organic compounds other than the essential proteins, fats, vitamins, and minerals. Although their absence will not cause illness, the presence of some secondary metabolites in a diet improves the quality of overall health. Secondary metabolites can include enzymes or other amino acids found in meat and also phytochemicals. Phytochemicals are a broad class of chemical compounds naturally found in plants. They may be vitamins, antioxidants, or other compounds that help create the taste, scent, and color of plants. For example, vanillin provides the scent of vanilla, while curcumin creates the vivid yellow color in turmeric.

Fresh ingredients in the right proportions are as valid for the dog's bowl as they are for our own plates; it just means separate pots on the stovetop. When we offer our pets fresh foods, they too can have meals that not only make a tail wag but also nourish and promote good health. In doing so, we are truly fulfilling our contract with our best friends.

Whose nose doesn't wrinkle at the thought of dog food? It doesn't smell all that great, and few of us would dare to put it in our own mouths. The nutritional analysis is mysterious and the ingredients are rarely related to foods that we know, leaving us standing in the pet food aisle pondering the difference between chicken by-products and chicken meal. The one assurance we are given is that it's complete and balanced.

The concern with commercial foods is that they are only complete and balanced for the obvious standards of vitamins, minerals, fats, proteins, and carbohydrates. There are thousands of compounds in foods, not just the short list of vitamins and minerals that we are familiar with, and more compounds are being discovered all the time. Take lycopene, for example. A few years ago few people had ever heard of lycopene or even the broader category of antioxidants. Then it was discovered that lycopene, found in red foods like tomatoes, watermelon, and papaya, might help prevent cancer in humans; recently it has been tested on dogs as well. Yet today when you read through the ingredients and analysis on any given bag, you see that it's only the standard vitamins and minerals that make it into commercial food. The antioxidants, phytochemicals, and secondary metabolites found abundantly in fresh foods that add to our health are not yet considered by pet food companies to be part of the canine "complete and balanced" equation, so they are left out of the bag.

One of the nutrients most likely to be deficient in a dog's diet is omega-3 fatty acid. We're learning that increasing omega-3s in our own diets can be beneficial, and they have been shown to improve skin conditions in dogs as well. The American Association of Feed Control Officials (AAFCO) sets the standard for the nutrient profiles in the pet food industry. Because the AAFCO does not recognize omega-3 fatty acids as an essential nutrient, pet food manufacturers are not required to include them. Will your dog perish without omega-3s in his diet? No, but the quality of his health can be improved by their inclusion. Without a standard, the marketing department can proudly tout "with added omega-3s," even when it's only a drop.

When a pet is diagnosed with cancer, people often ask me if it could be caused by the food they fed their dog. Cancer is a mystery—it pops up for its own reason, and can attack any part of a dog's body. The question is not whether commercial foods cause cancer, but rather whether they can do enough to prevent cancer. Our doctors urge us to eat fewer processed foods and less sugar, salt, fat, and meat for our own health. We are directed to the produce aisle to find fruits and vegetables that will supply us with carbohydrates for energy and vitamins and minerals to maintain our health. As an additional benefit, fresh foods also give us an abundant supply of antioxidants that build a foundation for a disease-free life. Antioxidants are just beginning to appear in pet foods, but too often they are limited to one or two of the thousands of antioxidants found in fresh foods. If you value fresh foods in your own diet, it's not much of a leap to see how they could benefit your dog as well.

"Nutrition is the key component of good health." It sounds so simple, but this was the most important sentence I read while researching canine nutrition. My experience with Jackson and hundreds of dogs has shown that the nutrition in real food can make a big impact on a dog's well-being. The meat loaves, stews, and slow cooker recipes in this book are simple and easy to make. You'll be surprised at how little effort they require. The dividends are huge; dogs always give positive reviews of their dining experience, and supplying a dog with fresh foods full of a large range of nutrients will keep that tail wagging for many happy years.

There is no one perfect food, meal, or method of feeding a dog. The possibilities are as numerous as the number of breeds in the American Kennel Club. Don't feel as if you need to do it all on your own. In fact, it will be easier for you and of greater benefit to your dog to supplement commercial food with a variety of fresh meals because your dog can receive vitamins and minerals from the highly supplemented commercial food and natural antioxidants from fresh foods.

The guidelines and recipes in this book have been developed to address any concerns that prevent us from sharing nature's bounty with our best friends. My focus is on first providing essential nutrients using basic foods, and then using two of my favorite dietary additions, Supplement Stew (page 14) and Eggshell Powder (page 15).

- If you just want to share some scraps from the kitchen counter, the "Foods Worth Sharing" section (page 28) will show the appropriate amounts for your dog and provide some recipes for foods you can both enjoy.
- The recipes beginning on page 36 will help you make dishes that you and your best friend can eat together with only small modifications.
- Show a little lovin' from the oven with delicious and nutritious morsels from the wide variety provided in the "Treats" section (page 47).
- Along with treats, the homemade delights in the "Cookies" section (page 73) can take training to another level, and they make great gifts.
- The "Meals" portion of the book (page 93) provides recipes that are balanced according to veterinary guidelines for macro nutrients (fats, carbohydrates, protein, and fiber) and include

guidelines for supplementing them to rival the complete and balanced nutrition found in commercial foods.

🐾 Some dogs have special needs due to medical conditions. The "Warm-Nose Meals for Ailing Dogs" section (page 133) includes recipes that are formulated to help a sick dog get back on his paws. It's worth a conversation with your veterinarian to determine whether these recipes are right for your dog.

🐾 Finally, talented pet photographer Alicia Dickerson Griffith illustrates our connection to our pets throughout this book in a photo essay titled "Your Best Friend." I hope you'll find something in these photos that reminds you of your own dog.

Fifteen thousand years after our first encounter, dogs remain our faithful companions and continue to prove their devotion in many ways. Share your own pictures and stories with me at www.dogfooddude.com. I hope both you and your pet enjoy the recipes in this book and that you share your affection for many years together.

Feed Your Best Friend Better,

Rick Woodford

BALANCING ACT:

NUTRIENTS IN A DOG'S DIET

Ensuring that the body receives the right amount of nutrients is important for both dogs and humans; it's only that the proportions are different for each species. Veterinarians are often cautious about endorsing home-cooked meals because they suspect the average recipe may be missing many of the vitamins and minerals necessary for good health. While there are some vitamins and minerals that need to be supplemented, some are actually manufactured within your dog's body and others can be met through modest servings of fresh foods. The following is an overview of the nutrients necessary for good health, their functions, and examples of how they are met through fresh foods.

PROTEIN

While the category of proteins earns most of the attention when talking about dog food, it's the amino acids that make up proteins that are truly important. In the digestive system, acids and enzymes break the proteins consumed down into amino acids, which are then utilized by the body to create cells, muscles, hormones, antibodies, blood, and even other amino acids. Of the 22 amino acids that a dog's body needs, 12 can be synthesized from other amino acids in the diet. The remaining 10 are called essential amino acids and need to be supplied in sufficient quantities for the body's functions. Protein sources are measured for how readily they are absorbed and utilized on a scale of biological value. Eggs earn the top rating of 94 percent, followed by fish at 76 percent, and beef at 74 percent; most grains earn values in the 60 percent range. The higher the quality of a protein source, the less protein needs to be consumed. When it comes to energy, the body's preferred source is fat and carbohydrates. When excess protein is consumed, some of the amino acids can be stored, although not to the extent of fat and carbohydrates. Too much protein puts additional stress on the kidneys, so dogs fighting illnesses should follow their veterinarian's recommendation for protein content. The recommendation for the average adult dog is 18 percent protein, whereas growing puppies, working dogs, and lactating bitches require 28 percent.

The essential amino acids all take part in the aforementioned bodily functions, but some have special purposes:

- Arginine—plays a role in cell replication and growth, so growing animals need more. Also aids in the detoxification of ammonia created by the digestion of proteins and stimulates the production of urine to carry away excess nitrogen.
- Histidine—plays a role in transporting oxygen through the blood.
- Isoleucine—only known function is in the creation of proteins.
- Leucine—assists in the synthesis of proteins and in preventing muscle from degrading.
- Lysine—diets heavier in grains have lower concentrations; however, the more protein in a diet, the more lysine is needed to utilize the protein consumed and synthesize other necessary proteins.

- Methionine—necessary for replication of DNA and RNA and for the synthesis of cystine, which is a major component of hair.
- Phenylalanine—contributes to the color of black hair, to creating the amino acid tyrosine, and to thyroid function.
- Threonine—supports healthy skin, healing of wounds, and the immune system.
- Tryptophan—believed to have an effect on the neurotransmitters that reduce aggression.
- Valine—active in the transportation of fats and the creation of milk.

The daily recommended amount of protein and the essential amino acids for a 40-pound dog can be met by ⅓ pound of chicken breast, which provides only 15 percent of the dog's necessary calories per day, leaving plenty of room for adding the right fats, vegetables, and even some grains in the diet.

Another amino acid, taurine, is synthesized by dogs using the methionine and cystine in the diet. Although there is not an established requirement for dogs, breeds that are predisposed to heart conditions, as well as Newfoundlands and cocker spaniels, can benefit from supplementation either by powdered formulations or through the inclusion of fish in the diet.

CARBOHYDRATES

While most nutrients have a set requirement, carbohydrates are the one nutrient for which it is really up to you as a pet owner to decide how much your dog receives. Dogs do not have a biological requirement for carbohydrates, and they're quite happy with a bowl full of meat for dinner. However, there are many reasons why including grains and vegetables are beneficial as part of a meal:

- As a source of energy, carbohydrates are more readily used than protein and lower in calories than fat.
- Carbohydrates slow digestion, allowing other nutrients more time to be absorbed and keeping your pet feeling fuller longer.
- Carbohydrates are a good source of essential vitamins, minerals, and the antioxidants that are not present in proteins or fats.
- Carbohydrates are less expensive than protein.

The growth and production of grains and vegetables have less of an impact on the environment, requiring less land, water, carbon emissions, and fossil fuels to deliver the same amount of calories as protein sources.

A concern with many commercial foods, especially those of lower quality, is that they are so high in carbohydrates because their protein sources originate largely from plant material as well. The amount of carbohydrates in your dog's diet is a choice for you to make, incorporating your own values and economics, and it doesn't have to be all or nothing. This book contains a variety of recipes for you to choose from that are grain free, low in carbohydrates, or contain a sensible balance of protein and carbohydrates.

FIBER

When a pet consumes carbohydrates, fiber rides along. Fiber remains largely undigested and slows the digestive system to balance the water content in the intestines, creating a healthy colon and increasing the amount of flora in the digestive tract to aid in the resistance to bacteria and intestinal disorders. Only a modest amount of fiber (less than 5 percent) is needed, because excess can encourage gas depending on the rate at which it is fermented.

FATS

Like carbohydrates and proteins, fats can cause obesity when consumed in excess. They have 225 percent as many calories per gram as either protein or carbohydrates. However, it's important to include fats in a diet because of their role in the absorption of fat-soluble vitamins A, D, E, and K; the production of hormones; the health of hair and skin; in increasing immunity; and as a source of energy. There are two types of essential fatty acids:

- 🐾 Omega-6 fatty acids are abundant in most diets that contain vegetable oils or animal fats; 1½ teaspoons of corn oil provides enough of the linoleic acid to meet a 40-pound dog's daily requirements. Omega-6 fatty acids also partner with zinc to create a healthy coat. However, an excess of omega-6 fatty acids (or more than 4 times the recommended daily allowance) can increase chemicals in the body that cause inflammation.
- 🐾 Omega-3 fatty acids are found in high concentrations in fish and fish oil; ¼ teaspoon of salmon oil or as little as 1 tablespoon of mackerel will provide enough to meet a 40-pound dog's daily requirement. Omega-3 fatty acids are strong anti-inflammatory agents that reduce the risk of heart disease, aid wound repair, and improve immunity. Despite these benefits, no requirement has been set by the AAFCO because there have been no studies to show that a deficiency causes issues. Because omega-3 fatty acids are worth including to aid your dog's overall health, there are recipes containing fish in each section of this book so that you can provide these nutritional powerhouses to your dog.

Your best friend doesn't grizzle about drizzle.

MINERALS

Minerals are inorganic chemical elements occurring naturally in the soil that are absorbed by plants and the animals that consume plant material. There are 12 minerals that have been subject to sufficient scientific research to demonstrate their daily requirement in a dog's diet.

Macro Minerals

- ❖ Calcium is the most abundant mineral in your dog's body, and is important for strong teeth and bones, the conduction of nerve impulses, blood coagulation, and muscular contraction. This mineral is the most likely to be deficient in home-cooked meals, and should be supplemented if more than 50 percent of your dog's food comes from your kitchen. It would take almost 5 cups of spinach or ⅓ pound of mozzarella cheese to meet a 40-pound dog's daily requirement. Rather than make a huge salad for your dog, you can use the Eggshell Powder recipe (page 15) to meet that same dog's requirement with just ¾ teaspoon.

- ❖ Phosphorus is just as busy as calcium, because they work in partnership and need to be balanced within the bloodstream. The majority of phosphorus is found in the skeleton. Elsewhere in the body phosphorus aids nerve impulses, maintains the pH balance in the blood, and assists in the metabolism of fats, proteins, and carbohydrates into energy. Although it takes ¾ pound of chicken to meet a 40-pound dog's daily requirements, deficiencies are rare because phosphorus is readily found in many foods, especially organ meats, fish, and poultry.

- ❖ Magnesium, like phosphorus and calcium, is found in greatest concentration in bones, but it is also found in organs and body fluids, where it assists in removing toxins from the body, aids heart function, and enables hormones in the body to function. Magnesium is widely available in plants and meat, but it would require ⅓ pound of salmon or 1½ cups of cooked quinoa to meet the daily requirement for a 40-pound dog. Deficiencies can cause epilepsy and increase the risk of heart disease, so it's a good idea to ensure that this is supplemented if your dog's diet is more than 50 percent homemade.

- ❖ Sodium maintains the balance of fluids in cells, which in turn assists in the delivery of nutrients and the removal of waste. A 40-pound dog needs about 230 milligrams of sodium per day, half of which can be found in ¼ cup of cottage cheese. Although many commercial foods provide more than 400 percent of a 40-pound dog's daily requirement (to enhance palatability), fresh foods like meat, fish, and cheese provide sufficient quantities to prevent deficiencies.

- ❖ Chloride maintains the pH balance of the body and is used in the digestion of protein. Chlorine is widely available in meats and plants; is especially high in table salt, seaweed, and tomatoes; and generally doesn't require supplementation because the requirements can be met when the intake of sodium is met.

- Potassium is found mostly in the fluids of cells. This mineral is essential for nerve transmissions and muscular contraction. Potatoes, yams, bananas, and whole grains are good sources, with 1 cup of yams supplying a full day's requirement for a 40-pound dog.
- Iron is mainly found in the blood. where it is used to transport oxygen to all cells in the body. Organ meats, beef, and fish are rich sources of iron; ⅓ pound of turkey giblets provides enough to meet the needs of a 40-pound dog.
- Iodine is required by thyroid hormones for growth and maintaining the metabolism. Because it's not stored in the body, a little bit is needed every day from foods like kelp, which can supply a full day's requirement for a 40-pound dog in as little as ⅛ teaspoon.
- Copper is necessary for healthy bone and connective tissue and for the formation of blood and the pigment in hair. Beef liver, quinoa, and millet are all great sources of copper, with just ½ ounce of liver providing a full day's requirement for a 40-pound dog.
- Manganese assists in the metabolizing of fat and carbohydrates, growth, reproduction, and the formation of bone. A 40-pound dog's daily requirement can be met with less than ¼ cup of oats.
- Zinc is widely used by more than 200 enzymes in the body that assist growth, healing, reproduction, and the metabolizing of carbohydrates and protein. The daily needs for a 40-pound dog can be met with ⅔ pound of lean ground beef.
- Selenium is essential to antioxidant activity within cells and is believed to help protect against cancer. Selenium also plays a role in the production of thyroid hormones, in reproduction, and in the immune system. Whole grains and organ meats can be great sources, but the strongest source is Brazil nuts, which meet a whole day's requirement for a 40-pound dog with one nut.

Micro Minerals

There are some micro minerals that are beneficial and required in only trace amounts. Because research on these minerals is lacking, they might not be supplemented in commercial foods, although they are found naturally in fresh foods.

- Boron contributes to the metabolism of minerals essential to bone growth, electrical impulses in the brain, and the regulation of the parathyroid hormone. It may also help alleviate symptoms of arthritis. Boron can be found in whole grains, vegetables, and fruits, with ½ cup of vegetables providing enough boron to meet a 40-pound dog's daily requirements.
- Chromium assists the body in using fat for energy and maintaining muscle tissue while enhancing the effect of insulin. Chromium is widely available in meat and plants, with nutritional yeast, grains, and wheat germ providing the greatest concentrations. One whole egg meets a 40-pound dog's daily requirement.

🐾 Molybdenum assists growth, the usage of iron, and in reproduction. Molybdenum is found in grains, dark leafy greens, and organ meats. It is estimated that one baby carrot can meet the nutritional needs of a 40-pound dog.

VITAMINS

Organic compounds required in the diet can be broken into two groups: fat-soluble vitamins (A, D, E, and K), which can be stored in the body's fat cells and organs, and water-soluble vitamins (B complex and C), which must be consumed on a regular basis to maintain bodily functions.

Vitamins A, D, E, and K

🐾 Vitamin A supports the immune system, bone and muscle growth, vision and health of the skin, and the body's internal linings. Vitamin A can be found in fish oils, liver, eggs, milk, and many root vegetables. A 40-pound dog's daily requirement can be met with ½ teaspoon of cod liver oil.

🐾 Vitamin D assists in the absorption of calcium and phosphorus to build healthy bones and aid in blood clotting and conduction of nerve impulses. Vitamin D can be found in fish oils, with ½ teaspoon of cod liver oil meeting a 40-pound dog's daily requirement.

🐾 Vitamin E is one of the most powerful antioxidants and is often used as a food preservative in commercial pet foods. Vitamin E also assists muscular health, nerve function, metabolizing fat, and hormone production. Vitamin E can be found in oils and some vegetables like spinach and butternut squash. The daily requirements for a 40-pound dog can be met with 1½ teaspoons of wheat germ oil.

🐾 Vitamin K can actually be synthesized in a dog's large intestines. Vitamin K assists in blood clotting and bone formation. Most dogs don't require supplementation unless they are taking antibiotics. Leafy green vegetables are strong sources of vitamin K, with 1 tablespoon of parsley providing enough to satisfy the daily requirements of a 40-pound dog.

B Vitamins

The B vitamins all assist in the metabolism of carbohydrates, fats, and proteins. They also make unique contributions to your dog's health:

🐾 Vitamin B_1 (thiamin) contributes to growth, neurological function, and the prevention of stool eating. B_1 is found in nutritional yeast, organ meats, and whole grains, with 1¼ teaspoons of nutritional yeast meeting the daily requirements of a 40-pound dog.

- Vitamin B_2 (riboflavin) supports the actions of other vitamins, and benefits eye and skin health. B_2 is found in organ meats and dairy products. A 40-pound dog's daily requirement can be met with the riboflavin found in 1 ounce of lamb liver.
- Vitamin B_3 (niacin) is especially important for energy metabolism and maintaining strong muscles. B_3 can be found in chicken, fish, and nutritional yeast, with 2 ounces of chicken breast meeting the daily requirements of a 40-pound dog.
- Vitamin B_5 (pantothenic acid) supports the production of hormones, and aids in digestion and reproduction. B_5 is found in meats, eggs, nutritional yeast, and dark green vegetables. The daily requirement for a 40-pound dog can be met with 1 tablespoon of nutritional yeast.
- Vitamin B_6 (pyridoxine) aids red blood cell production and the function of scores of enzymes. B_6 is found in meats and nutritional yeast. Two ounces of chicken breast can meet the daily requirements for a 40-pound dog.
- Vitamin B_{12} (cobalamin) is necessary for red blood cell production, nerve transmission, and heart health. B_{12} can only be found in meat products like poultry, fish, and organ meats. Two ounces of turkey giblets can provide the daily B_{12} requirement of a 40-pound dog.
- Biotin helps transform amino acids into muscle and improves the health of both skin and hair. One reason to avoid feeding raw eggs to dogs is that the avidin in the egg white prevents biotin from being absorbed. Biotin can be found in egg yolks, liver, and nutritional yeast. The daily requirements of a 40-pound dog can be met with 1 egg yolk.
- Folic acid makes important contributions to the growth and division of cells, red blood cell production, and prevention of birth abnormalities during pregnancy. Folic acid is found in green leafy vegetables, liver, and nutritional yeast, as well as foods like rice and pasta, which are often enriched with vitamins and minerals. One-half cup of cooked white rice provides enough folic acid to meet the requirements of a 40-pound dog.
- Choline is not a true vitamin, but it acts much like the other B vitamins in the metabolism of fats and is utilized to create nerve chemicals for brain function. Eggs and organ meats can provide choline, but it would require 4 eggs or 2 tablespoons of soy lecithin to meet the requirements of a 40-pound dog. It's recommended that supplementations you provide include choline.

Vitamin C

- Vitamin C (ascorbic acid) acts as an antioxidant, and assists collagen and hormone production and the growth and maintenance of tissue cells. Fruits and vegetables are high in vitamin C, but because dogs can synthesize vitamin C in their liver, no supplementation is generally required for healthy dogs.

You may recognize a lot of these nutrients as components of your own healthy diet, but a dog's nutritional needs are certainly different from our own. The accompanying example illustrates the nutritional requirements of a dog and a human girl, both weighing 50 pounds and requiring the same amount of calories per day. Dogs require a higher amount of nutrients such as calcium, selenium, B vitamins, copper, and zinc. Commercial foods add these in as supplements in order to achieve "complete and balanced nutrition." We can achieve the same results by providing a multivitamin and a balanced meal with the additional benefits of fresh foods.

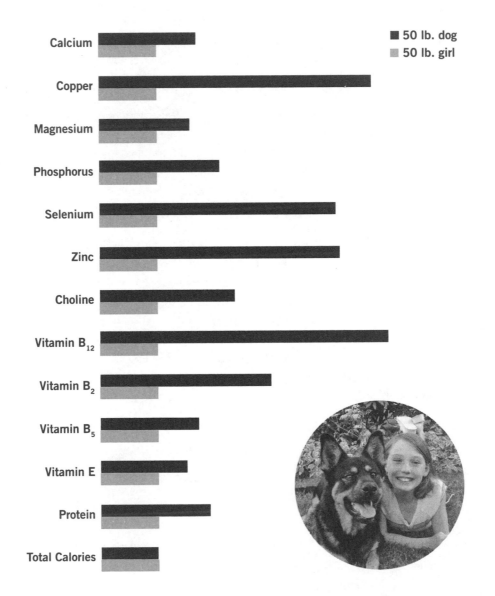

■ 50 lb. dog
■ 50 lb. girl

Calcium
Copper
Magnesium
Phosphorus
Selenium
Zinc
Choline
Vitamin B$_{12}$
Vitamin B$_2$
Vitamin B$_5$
Vitamin E
Protein
Total Calories

Well-developed and supplemented home-cooked meals are even approved by the *Small Animal Clinical Nutrition* volume sitting on your veterinarian's desk. Serving your dog an occasional meal without supplementation won't do any harm, but prolonged feeding without supplementation can lead to deficiencies that can create problems for the skin and hair, eyes, skeleton, and even the functioning of internal organs.

Supplementation can be as easy as adding some Eggshell Powder (page 15) and a multivitamin to your dog's cooked food each day. If you'd prefer to have more nutrition come from natural sources, my Supplement Stew recipe (page 14) relies first on food sources and then adds a vitamin–mineral tablet and the Eggshell Powder to round out the nutrition. Supplement Stew can be added to any recipe in the book unless otherwise noted for dogs with specific ailments.

UP TO 50 PERCENT OF THE TOTAL DIET FROM HOME-COOKED MEALS

Commercial foods are often supplemented at more than 200 percent of the recommended daily allowance for vitamins and minerals.

Supplementation with one of the methods below is optional but recommended.

MORE THAN 50 PERCENT OF THE TOTAL DIET FROM HOME-COOKED MEALS

Supplementation with one of the methods below is highly recommended.

Add 2½ teaspoons of Eggshell Powder to finished recipes after they have cooled and provide a daily vitamin according to manufacturer's directions.

or

Mix ⅓ cup Supplement Stew with ⅔ cup water and add to finished recipes after they have cooled.

Your best friend orders anchovies.

SUPPLEMENT STEW

Your dog will love the meat and veggies in the meal recipes, and those will provide many antioxidants, vitamins, and minerals. However, as great as real ingredients are for your dog, no specific combination can meet all of your dog's nutritional needs. The next source I look at to provide vitamins and minerals is natural ingredients. Collected here is a powerful supporting group of foods that are easy to assemble and add to your dog's meals.

- Brazil nuts are loaded with selenium, which, when combined with vitamin E, acts as an antioxidant to prevent cell damage and support a healthy heart, joints, skin, and coat.
- Soy lecithin brings choline and linoleic acid to the diet for transporting fatty acids out of the liver and contributing to proper nerve function.
- Nutritional yeast is packed with B vitamins, which help to metabolize and assist the body in utilizing all the other nutrients for growth and energy.
- Eggshell Powder (page 15) provides the calcium necessary to balance the phosphorus in your dog's diet, build strong bones and muscles, and assist in the vital functions of blood coagulation, muscle contraction, and transmission of nerve impulses.
- Kelp provides marine minerals, including potassium, magnesium, calcium, and iron and is an excellent source of iodine, which supports thyroid function and regulating your dog's metabolism.
- Yogurt provides bacteria, which are beneficial to your dog's digestive system. Plain low-fat yogurt is the best choice because it's low in calories and doesn't contain added sugar.
- Apple cider vinegar should be purchased with the "mother," which is a cloudy sediment at the bottom of the bottle that contains vitamins and minerals. Although the amount of the minerals is negligible, apple cider vinegar also has antiseptic properties that benefit your dog from the inside out. This vinegar can be used on the outside as well, for cleaning ears with yeast infections (mix ½ teaspoon vinegar with ¼ cup water, then dampen a towel to gently clean ears).
- Salmon and cod liver oil are both high in omega-3 fatty acids and can be used interchangeably, although I prefer salmon oil and so do our dogs. If you're using cod liver oil, do not use flavored oil because many dogs dislike the taste of the added orange or lemon flavorings. Fish oil has powerful anti-inflammatory properties and helps to provide a shiny, healthy coat. Salmon oil can usually be purchased at pet stores, and cod liver oil is widely available in pharmacies.
- Multivitamin tablets ensure all other vitamins and minerals are supplied. I use the One A Day Men's formula because it doesn't have excess iron and is a good match for dogs. You can also use multivitamin formulations made for dogs, if desired.
- Mix ⅓ cup Supplement Stew (recipe follows) with ⅔ cup water, then blend into any finished recipe once the recipe has cooled. The water will help to evenly distribute the nutrition throughout the food and keep the calories per cup of food consistent.

SUPPLEMENT STEW

4 multivitamin tablets (One A Day Men's preferred)

6 Brazil nuts

½ cup soy lecithin granules

1 tablespoon nutritional yeast

3 tablespoons Eggshell Powder (recipe follows)

1 tablespoon dried kelp or seaweed powder

½ cup plain low-fat yogurt

¼ cup apple cider vinegar (shake vigorously before measuring)

¼ cup salmon or cod liver oil

Crush the vitamin tablets individually and add to a food processor with the Brazil nuts. Pulse for 5 seconds, or until the vitamins are reduced to a fine powder and the nuts resemble small meal.

Add the soy lecithin, nutritional yeast, Eggshell Powder, and kelp to the food processor, and then layer the yogurt, vinegar, and fish oil on top. (This helps to prevent any dust from forming when you open the food processor.)

Pulse the mixture for an additional 15 seconds and then divide into 4 portions of ⅓ cup each for adding to finished recipes.

Store in the refrigerator for up to 4 days or in the freezer for up to 1 month.

YIELD: 1⅓ cups, enough to supplement 4 meal recipes

If you prefer to use other sources of calcium for supplementation, it requires much more to achieve the same effect as the Eggshell Powder. In the Supplement Stew recipe, the 3 tablespoons of Eggshell Powder provide 16,200 mg of calcium and almost no phosphorus.

Some common calcium supplements and their equivalent amounts for use in the Supplement Stew:

KAL Dolomite Powder: *This product contains 1,100 milligrams per teaspoon and no additional phosphorus. The lower amount of calcium requires ¼ cup when used in the Supplement Stew.*

Bonemeal: *Different brands contain varied amounts of calcium and phosphorus. In most cases, half of the calcium is used in balancing out the additional phosphorus included in the Supplement Stew. Average bonemeal contains 960 milligrams of calcium and 360 milligrams of phosphorus in each teaspoon, which means that only 540 milligrams of calcium are provided, requiring ⅔ cup in the Supplement Stew recipe.*

Calcium carbonate: *In powdered form, about 1,200 milligrams of calcium are provided in each teaspoon without any additional phosphorus. Use ¼ cup in the Supplement Stew recipe.*

Seaweed Calcium *is made from calcified seaweed and also contains magnesium, zinc, iodine, and selenium. Use ⅓ cup in the Supplement Stew recipe.*

These calcium supplements are widely available at pet stores, pharmacies, and through the Internet.

Eggshell Powder

One of the most important supplements you'll need to add to your dog's meals is calcium. If dogs had the ability to chew on a good bone every day, they would be scraping off bits of bone that then would be broken down in their body and used to strengthen their own bones and teeth. It's the job of the parathyroid to regulate the amount of calcium and phosphorus in the blood. If a diet is deficient in calcium, the parathyroid will go looking for it in your dog's bones. When the parathyroid starts secreting extra hormones in order to balance the calcium-to-phosphorus ratio, it creates a condition known as secondary hyperparathyroidism. This disorder can cause permanent damage to the skeletal system, arthritis, and even broken bones. Extra calcium will be excreted in the urine, but while it's in the body, excess calcium inhibits the absorption of phosphorus. So don't overdo a good thing.

By diverting eggshells from the compost bin you can have an inexpensive and easy solution to providing your dog the appropriate amount of calcium. It requires only a couple of teaspoons of Eggshell Powder to balance out the phosphorus in most diets, and this recipe will make about 12 teaspoons, each with about 1,800 milligrams of calcium.

12 eggshells, cleaned and dried

Once clean and dry, eggshells can be left at room temperature in an airtight container until you save enough to make a batch.

Preheat the oven to 300°F.

Spread the eggshells evenly on a baking sheet and bake for 5 to 7 minutes. The eggshells will still be mostly white or brown, but might have a light tint, which is okay. Baking eggshells any longer can produce an unpleasant smell.

Allow the eggshells to cool, then grind in a blender or clean coffee grinder for 1 minute, or until you achieve a very fine powder with no sharp edges.

Store at room temperature in an airtight container for up to 2 months.

YIELD: 12 teaspoons

DETERMINING PORTION SIZE

How much you feed your dog is just as important as what you feed your dog. The first step in defining your dog's caloric requirement is to evaluate your dog's current health. There are three components that will determine just how much food you put into the bowl: your dog's activity level, weight, and body type.

Pet food manufacturers suggest adjusting feeding portions according to a dog's activity level. However, there really hasn't been much definition put behind what constitutes an active dog—until now.

Each new customer who subscribed to my Dog Stew service filled out an extensive pet profile, with a good part of it concentrating on the dog's condition and activity level. Knowing this information and monitoring each dog's weight, overall physical health, and caloric intake helped me develop a more definitive classification for activity levels.

EXTRA-ACTIVE DOGS

An extra-active dog plays hard. You know if you have an extra-active dog, because you are exhausted just keeping up with him.

- Two long (30-plus minute) walks per day

and at least one of the following:

- Running with a family member 3-plus times a week
- Ball chasers that spend a few hours a week scrambling around chasing a ball
- Young dogs who live in homes with young children or multiple dogs and are constantly playing
- Dogs who play hard at the dog park 3-plus times per week for a minimum of 30 minutes

ACTIVE DOGS

The active dog engages in a fair amount of activity, enough to leave him satisfied but not exhausted at the end of the day.

- At least two good (20-plus minutes) walks per day

and at least one of the following:

- Jogging with a family member at least a couple of times a week
- Hiking or long (2-plus hours) walks at least once a week
- Visits the dog park a couple of times a week but does not engage in excessive play
- Middle-aged dogs who live in multiple dog houses or with young children and are up and around more than they are resting

INACTIVE DOGS

The inactive dog is your basic couch potato. If you have to sit on the floor to watch TV because the dog owns the couch for 20 hours a day, you have yourself a couch potato.

- Less than 40 minutes of walking per day
- Senior dogs or middle-aged dogs with reduced activity

The next step is to get your dog on a scale. If your dog is small enough, you can weigh yourself, make a note of your weight, and then weigh yourself holding your dog. Subtract your weight to find your dog's weight. Otherwise, make a trip to your veterinarian and ask to use his or her scale. While you are there, ask your veterinarian to evaluate your pet as well to determine the ideal weight for your dog's breed and body type.

Use the charts that follow to determine how many calories your dog should ideally be consuming per day. If your dog falls somewhere in between activity levels, adjust the calories accordingly. Just be sure not to be too generous. When you've found the ideal number of calories, write it down, because the next step is to determine whether any adjustments need to be made.

Calorie recommendations from commercial pet food companies vary widely, and there are multiple methods of calculating caloric requirements. My recommendations are based upon feeding fresh meals to hundreds of dogs, monitoring their weight, and adjusting portion sizes, which I was able to control with precision. These recommendations represent those for an indoor, neutered dog and are conservative to prevent excess weight gain and to include a small allowance for treats.

Knowing your pet's weight, the next step is to determine whether your dog's curves are in the right proportion.

Pets who are obese (about 45 percent of our pets) are more likely to develop diabetes, arthritis, hip dysplasia, ligament or tendon injuries, or have strokes, breathing difficulties, and skin problems. Some people have a hard time feeding their dog less because the dog enjoys eating, and food is one way that we show our love. However, overweight dogs will have a reduced life expectancy, and their quality of life is reduced by these symptoms. Homemade foods can be a healthy way to help your pet slim down because their higher water content provides added bulk without the added calories.

At the other end of the scale, underweight dogs are less likely to be able to fight off parasites and disease. Some factors that may cause a dog to be underweight are underfeeding, poor nutritional value in the food, parasites, diabetes, or other diseases. If your pet is underweight or especially if your dog is thin, you should contact your veterinarian to rule out any underlying causes.

To evaluate your dog's body type, first stand over the top of your standing dog. The ideal would be to see curves that go in at the hips, not curves that go out. For the second step, take a look at your dog from the side (you may have to get down on the floor for this part) and check out your dog's stomach. Again, we're looking for a curve that goes in, not a curve that goes out. If your dog has a very fluffy coat, try this examination while giving your dog a bath. Next, feel along your dog's rib cage. You should feel your dog's ribs underneath a thin layer of skin and fat. Certain breeds, like Greyhounds and Bulldogs, can be difficult to judge, but your veterinarian can always supply an objective opinion.

AVERAGE CALORIE REQUIREMENTS PER DAY

WEIGHT IN LBS	4	6	8	10	12	14	15
EXTRA-ACTIVE	210	250	350	410	470	530	560
ACTIVE	180	210	300	350	400	450	470
INACTIVE	130	160	230	270	310	340	360

WEIGHT IN LBS	16	18	20	25	30	35	40
EXTRA-ACTIVE	590	640	700	820	940	1060	1170
ACTIVE	500	540	590	700	800	900	990
INACTIVE	380	410	450	530	610	680	750

WEIGHT IN LBS	45	50	55	60	65	70	75
EXTRA-ACTIVE	1,280	1,380	1,490	1,590	1,690	1,780	1,880
ACTIVE	1,080	1,170	1,260	1,340	1,430	1,510	1,590
INACTIVE	820	890	960	1,020	1,080	1,150	1,210

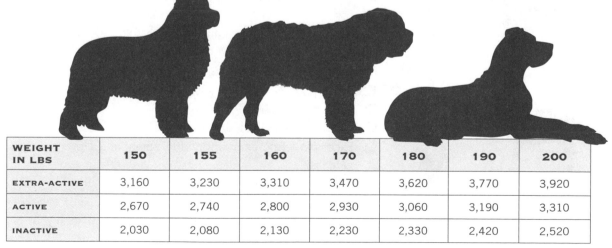

WEIGHT IN LBS	80	85	90	95	100	105	110
EXTRA-ACTIVE	1,970	2,060	2,150	2,240	2,330	2,420	2,500
ACTIVE	1,670	1,740	1,820	1,900	1,970	2,040	2,120
INACTIVE	1,270	1,320	1,380	1,440	1,500	1,550	1,610

WEIGHT IN LBS	115	120	125	130	135	140	145
EXTRA-ACTIVE	2,590	2,670	2,750	2,830	2,920	3,000	3,080
ACTIVE	2,190	2,260	2,330	2,400	2,470	2,530	2,600
INACTIVE	1,660	1,720	1,770	1,820	1,870	1,930	1,980

WEIGHT IN LBS	150	155	160	170	180	190	200
EXTRA-ACTIVE	3,160	3,230	3,310	3,470	3,620	3,770	3,920
ACTIVE	2,670	2,740	2,800	2,930	3,060	3,190	3,310
INACTIVE	2,030	2,080	2,130	2,230	2,330	2,420	2,520

EMACIATED

- • Obvious waist and abdominal tuck
- • No fat cover over ribs
- • Ribs, spine, and hip bones can be felt, similar to the feel of the bones on the inside of your palm where your fingers connect.

UNDERWEIGHT

- * Waist and abdominal tuck are easily visible
- • Minimal fat cover over ribs
- • Ribs, spine, and hips are easily felt and visible, similar to the feel of the bones on the back of your hand

IDEAL

- Waist visible behind ribs
- Abdominal tuck rises above ribs
- Thin layer of fat cover over ribs
- Ribs, spine, and hips can be felt under slight fat cover, similar to the feel of the bones on the outside of your wrist, at the top of your forearm

OVERWEIGHT

- Waist visible but is not prominent
- Apparent abdominal tuck, but does not rise much above rib cage
- Ribs, spine, and hips can be slightly felt under excessive fat cover

OBESE

- Waist is not visible
- No abdominal tuck visible
- Excessive fat cover prevents ribs, spine, and hip bones from being felt

If your dog needs to lose a little weight, see page 164 for instructions on how to reduce portions while ensuring that you keep your pet from feeling as if he's on a diet.

FOODS TO SHARE

SCRAMBLED EGG

SWEET POTATO FRIES FOR SHARING

SALMON PATTIES

DUTCH BABY PANCAKE

BAKED APPLES

BLUEBERRY PANCAKES

KEBABS FOR DOGS

TUNA SANDWICH LEFTOVERS

CHEESE CHIPS

When you're making your own meals, do you find yourself being watched by puppy-dog eyes and a tail that wags slowly in anticipation? Dogs have practiced that look for millennia; it's practically handed down generation after generation in their genetic code—because it works. The quickest method of shutting down that Pavlovian puddle of drool gathering on the floor is to provide a bite or two of the foods you're preparing. Sharing is not a sign of weakness or spoiling your dog. As long as foods shared are safe and in appropriate amounts there's no reason to withhold from our dogs fresh, wholesome foods and the nutrients they provide.

In this section you'll find ingredients to avoid, ingredients to use with caution, and ingredients that are fantastic choices for sharing off the cutting board or as supplements to your dog's meals. Each ingredient includes portion sizes for dogs of various weights, so you can prevent any digestive upset or over-supplementation of any nutrient. Yes, you can feed your dog off your cutting board; just don't feed your dog off your plate. Once a dish reaches the dinner table it's filled with salt, pepper, fat, onion, or other ingredients that can adversely affect your dog.

Also included are a few recipes that can be shared with your dog with slight modifications or by setting some aside while you prepare your own. These recipes only include ingredients and quantities that are safe for your dog. Because these recipes are intended as additions to your dog's regular meals, serving sizes reflect a snack-size portion.

Have fun sharing, but at least have your dog sit before you hand over the goods.

FOODS TO AVOID

There is much debate about which foods are good for dogs and which are not. However, there are some foods known to be harmful to pets. Maybe your dog has eaten a grape or raisin before without incident, but you never know which grape will be the tipping point. The liver stores a variety of vitamin and minerals, and we still don't know how much it stores of some chemicals in foods that are dangerous to dogs. With so many different foods free of controversy that your dog is sure to enjoy, don't put your pet at risk with these foods.

ALCOHOLIC BEVERAGES

There's nothing funny about giving a dog sips of beer or other alcoholic beverages. Your dog is the ultimate lightweight, and just a little bit of alcohol can cause vomiting, seizures, and even death.

CHOCOLATE

The mixture of caffeine, theobromine, and theophylline in any type of chocolate product can be toxic because they stimulate your pet's nervous system. Cocoa powder can have up to twice as much theobromine as other types of chocolate. Contact your veterinarian immediately if your dog consumes chocolate products.

Carob is a safe food for dogs, but recipes using this ingredient have not been included because it's not an ingredient most people commonly have in their kitchen, and it has few benefits for dogs. Also, if we're trying to keep our dogs from eating chocolate, why give them a chocolate-like substance?

FAT AND SKIN

Including oils and some animal fat in your dog's diet is essential to good health. What's not good for your dog is what you left on your plate after enjoying a delicious steak. That steak fat is not only a big fat bomb waiting to explode, it's also been spiced with salt and pepper, making it more likely to cause diarrhea, vomiting, or possibly pancreatitis (in which case you get a generous supply of both symptoms). The same logic applies to Thanksgiving turkey skin, which causes hundreds of pancreatitis cases every year and has caused lean turkey meat to be guilty by association. On its own, turkey is a lean meat that is safe for dogs. Recipes included in this book contain fat and skin as part of a planned diet in amounts that are safe for your dog.

GRAPES AND RAISINS

The flesh of both grapes and raisins contain an unknown toxin that can damage the kidneys and cause kidney failure. As little as 3 or 4 grapes could cause problems for a 50-pound dog. There have been no problems associated with grape seed extract, which is often given as an antioxidant supplement because the offending toxin is water soluble and not found in the seeds.

MACADAMIA AND OTHER NUTS

When you come back from Hawaii, put these tasty treats up high. Macadamia nuts contain a toxin that may affect the digestive and nervous systems and may cause vomiting, muscle tremors, or elevated heart rate. Contact your veterinarian if your dog should get into these nuts.

Walnuts are also reported to be dangerous because of mold. Peanuts and Brazil nuts, however, can be safe for your dog as long as your dog tolerates them and you feed only in small amounts.

MOLDY FOODS

If it's not good enough for you (including cheese with questionable mold), then it's not good enough for your pet.

NUTMEG AND MACE

These are seemingly innocent spices used in many baked goods and savory dishes, but they can affect your dog's central nervous system, causing digestive issues, vomiting, seizures, or even death.

ONIONS

Whether it is fresh, dried, or powdered, the thiosulphate in onions can damage red blood cells and cause Heinz body anemia. If it has onions in it, it doesn't go in your dog; this includes most store-bought broths and a large portion of prepared foods. If your dog has eaten a food with onions and begins to show unusual symptoms (vomiting, blood in urine or stool, diarrhea, weakness), contact your veterinarian for a blood test. On the positive side, cooking for your dog is tear free.

BLACK PEPPER

Your dog doesn't need pepper to make food taste good, so there's no reason to add it when you're cooking for your pet. Steer clear of prepared foods with pepper because they can irritate your dog's digestive system.

PITS FROM FRUIT

Pits can cause obstructions in the digestive track, so if your dog happens to like apricots, mango, peaches, or plums, be sure to remove the pit prior to serving, regardless of your dog's size.

RAW SALMON AND TROUT

Not all salmon and trout are created equal because not all habitats have issues with the fluke flatworm. Raw salmon and trout from the Pacific Northwest should not be fed to your dog because it can be potentially fatal. Symptoms normally appear within a week of feeding these fish to your dog. Well-cooked and processed fish is safe for your dog to eat and a great source of omega-3 fatty acids.

SALT AND SALTY FOODS

There is enough sodium in a natural diet to meet your pet's daily requirement, so there is little reason to add more. Too much salt can cause electrolyte imbalances. Processed foods that we enjoy are usually packed with a great deal of sodium and shouldn't be shared, as one salty chip in a Yorkie's stomach can cause big issues.

YEAST DOUGH

Imagine eating a yeasty dinner roll without it being cooked. Inside your warm stomach the dough continues to expand and produce gas, leading to discomfort and possible rupture of your digestive system. The same goes for your dog, so be sure to place rising dough out of your counter surfer's reach.

FOODS TO APPROACH WITH CAUTION

Some foods will come down to a matter of choice and the ability of your dog's digestive system to tolerate them. You can never go wrong by soliciting your veterinarian's opinion.

BONES

Dogs love chewing on bones. They are mentally stimulating, they are great for a dog's teeth, and the small bits of bone a dog scrapes off are a good source of calcium.

The issue with all types of bones is that they can splinter, cause perforation or obstruction in the digestive tract, or fracture your dog's teeth. Most dogs should be able to digest a small amount of bone, but before allowing unsupervised consumption, you should be fully aware of how fast your dog can break into a bone. Take bones away from your dog and inspect every 15 minutes; if you notice large pieces missing or cracks in the bone, it's time to throw it away. Do not allow your pet to gnaw bones to a size that they could swallow.

Poultry bones should be avoided because their porous nature makes them likely to splinter. Instead, look for beef marrowbones; they have a delicious center filling and the bones are thicker, so they are less likely to splinter.

Cooking destroys the structural integrity of all bones, making them more likely to fracture, so cooked bones should never be fed to a dog.

MILK PRODUCTS

In our house, dogs get a very small splash of reduced-fat milk or plain low-fat yogurt in the morning; we call it their puppy coffee. Every once in a while, we give the dogs small pieces of cheese or scrape out the cheese grater into a lucky dog's bowl. However, many dogs lose their ability to process lactose shortly after being weaned (just like some humans do). Our dogs consume dairy products without issue only because we keep it to a minimum. I've talked to many people whose dog has suddenly had a bout of diarrhea, and many times it goes back to the overfeeding of cheese. If you know your dog can eat cheese in small amounts, then it's okay to share; refer to the section on foods worth sharing starting on page 28 to learn the appropriate serving size.

AVOCADOS

The leaves and pit of the avocado contain the toxin persin, known to cause vomiting, diarrhea, and gastrointestinal irritation. The greatest concern comes from Guatemalan avocados, and less from California Hass avocados. Avocado flesh is rich in nutrients and has essential fatty acids that can help improve your dog's skin and coat, but excessive fat intake can cause some of the above digestive symptoms as well, so limit the amount you feed to your dog.

LIVER

Whether the liver in question is beef, chicken, or something more exotic, dogs will do just about anything for liver. Liver is rich in vitamins A and D; so rich, in fact, that it should be no more than 5 percent of a dog's diet. This makes it better as a treat or snack rather than as a meal. (See the recipes for Loyalty Liver Paté, page 51, and Robert's Liver Treats, page 49.) Even when providing treats, do so in moderation to avoid digestive upset. Terriers in particular can accumulate excessive amounts of copper in their livers, resulting in hepatitis, lethargy, vomiting, and weight loss, so treats with liver should be avoided altogether for these dogs.

FOODS WORTH SHARING

From an early age we're taught to share, but not with our dogs. While you're preparing your own meals, be on the lookout for foods that can be safe additions to your dog's bowl and circumvent the garbage can by using scraps as snacks. When I'm cooking my own meals, there are eight eyes watching my every move. They know that if they stay in their appointed area, I'll figure out something to sneak into their bowls. One day we were baking pies and it was small pieces of organic pears. A few days later I was making pear butter with the remaining fruit and decided to make some dried pear strips with the skins. The dogs wouldn't touch the raw skins but went crazy for the dried jerky. Sometimes it just requires a little creativity when introducing new foods.

The amounts given here are "Reasonable Daily Amounts"; think of this as the RDA for the canine set. Feeding less than that is certainly okay, because these amounts are in addition to what you're already feeding your dog. The RDAs are set so as not to disrupt the amount of fat, vitamins and minerals, fiber, and calories in your dog's normal diet. Following the RDAs will allow you to treat your dog and avoid digestive upset.

All quantities are given in standard kitchen measurements, but you don't need to pull out the measuring cups every time you feed your dog a snack. A tablespoon doesn't mean a heaping tablespoon; you're aiming to dish out a moderately level amount equivalent to the large spoon you would use to eat soup. A teaspoon should be close to the teaspoon used to stir cream into your coffee.

If you're giving your dog multiple snacks throughout the day, aim for variety, such as a vegetable in the morning, a small piece of bread in the afternoon, and a piece of meat in the evening. Mix and match according to what works for you and what your dog enjoys; just practice moderation.

The amounts in this section are less than 10 percent of the average dog's caloric intake. With some of the RDAs (and especially when you get to the part about cheese on page 32), you may think it's a stingy amount, but it's in your dog's best interest. Tips are provided to help you extend the experience rather than your dog's waistline.

Any time you give your dog something new, do so in small increments to see how your pet's palate and stomach tolerate it. So the first time you give your dog a new food, use about one-quarter of the reasonable daily amount and then move up to one-half the next time, and so on. If you notice any foods that aren't tolerated, discontinue them.

If your dog simply turns his nose up, try again when he's really hungry. We repeatedly offered the dogs banana, only to be rejected, and finally Chloe (who would previously only eat meat or cheese snacks) tried a slice and deemed it worthy of her notice. Now every day Chloe waits patiently for a slice. For some dogs, new textures are exciting, but other dogs may need some coaxing. If your dog won't eat a carrot, for example, try shredding carrots into the food. Once a dog starts learning that a new food is okay, he's more likely to try it on its own.

FRUITS

Apples and Pears

Dogs generally prefer red apples to green. Try a slice, and if your dog raises his nose away, then you might want to try removing the peel. Because apple seeds contain cyanide, apple cores should not be given to dogs.

10-POUND DOG	20-POUND DOG	40-POUND DOG	60-POUND DOG	80-POUND DOG
⅛ apple	⅓ apple	½ apple	⅔ apple	1 whole apple (cored)

Bananas

It's a bit of a double standard, but I won't eat a spotted (ripe) banana. I will, however, sneak them into the dogs' bowls along with their meal. Whether you're making breakfast or banana splits, feel free to add this potassium-packed powerhouse to your pooch's bowl. Bananas should be ripe, not green; otherwise your dog will have a difficult time digesting them.

10-POUND DOG	20-POUND DOG	40-POUND DOG	60-POUND DOG	80-POUND DOG
1-inch slice	2-inch slice	⅓ banana	½ banana	⅔ banana

Mangos and Papayas

Did you read about Marley in *Marley & Me*? Although he was a lot of trouble, he loved mangos. Both mangos and papayas are filled with antioxidants and enzymes that assist digestion.

10-POUND DOG	20-POUND DOG	40-POUND DOG	60-POUND DOG	80-POUND DOG
2 teaspoons	2 tablespoons	¼ cup	⅓ cup	½ cup

Melons

Watermelon or cantaloupe can help your dog cool down in the summer. Give your dog cubes of melon, but not the rind, which might cause an upset stomach.

10-POUND DOG	20-POUND DOG	40-POUND DOG	60-POUND DOG	80-POUND DOG
2 tablespoons	¼ cup	½ cup	⅔ cup	1 cup

Oranges

There are a few dogs who enjoy citrus fruit; if yours is one, it's okay to share this vitamin C–packed fruit; just peel it and give your dog the appropriate number of sections.

10-POUND DOG	20-POUND DOG	40-POUND DOG	60-POUND DOG	80-POUND DOG
1 section	2 sections	3 sections	4 sections	6 sections

Plums and Apricots

During the summer, Baxter goes absolutely insane when he smells a plum nearby. Some dogs love the sweet, juicy taste; but remember to remove the pit.

10-POUND DOG	20-POUND DOG	40-POUND DOG	60-POUND DOG	80-POUND DOG
⅛ plum	⅓ plum	½ plum	⅔ plum	1 whole plum

VEGETABLES

Broccoli

Here's a vegetable that's loaded with vitamins but has a pretty bad rap for dogs. Broccoli contains isothio-cyanate, which can upset your dog's digestive system in large doses. Few of us, however, would attempt to give our dogs a whole head of broccoli every day. In small amounts, this vegetable can be a good addition to your dog's diet. You're probably not going to eat those broccoli stalks anyway, so let your dog gnaw on them; or chop them up, lightly steam, and add a small amount to your dog's food.

10-POUND DOG	20-POUND DOG	40-POUND DOG	60-POUND DOG	80-POUND DOG
2 teaspoons	2 tablespoons	¼ cup	⅓ cup	½ cup

Carrots

Not only are carrots high in vitamins but they also provide a good chewing activity. If your dog won't eat a whole carrot, try grating it and mixing it with a meal, or steaming it.

10-POUND DOG	20-POUND DOG	40-POUND DOG	60-POUND DOG	80-POUND DOG
1 baby carrot	2 baby carrots	3 baby carrots	4 baby carrots	5 baby carrots

Green Beans and Snap Peas

Our dogs love these green vegetables, so we sneak them a couple while preparing meals. It's okay for snacking, but in larger quantities, they should be grated or pulsed in the food processor to break down the cellular structure.

10-POUND DOG	20-POUND DOG	40-POUND DOG	60-POUND DOG	80-POUND DOG
2 whole beans or pods	3 whole beans or pods	4 whole beans or pods	5 whole beans or pods	6 whole beans or pods

Bell Peppers (Red, Yellow, Orange)

The test subjects in our home definitely prefer the rosy hues of red, yellow, or orange bell peppers over green bell peppers. Remove all the seeds and chop or dice.

10-POUND DOG	20-POUND DOG	40-POUND DOG	60-POUND DOG	80-POUND DOG
2 teaspoons	4 teaspoons	2 tablespoons	3 tablespoons	¼ cup

Parsley

If you have extra parsley, whether it be the head or the stems, curly or flat leaf, chop it up finely and store in the fridge. Add some daily to your dog's dish to aid digestion and sweeten that doggy breath.

10-POUND DOG	20-POUND DOG	40-POUND DOG	60-POUND DOG	80-POUND DOG
2 teaspoons	4 teaspoons	2 tablespoons	3 tablespoons	¼ cup

Potatoes

This potassium powerhouse is a great treat because it's low in calories, is a great source of dietary fiber, and has as much vitamin C as a tomato. Whether you're making potatoes mashed or boiled, keep the skins on, remove any eyes, and remove your dog's portion before you salt them. Do not use any potatoes with a green hue to the skin because that green tint indicates the presence of solanine, which is toxic to dogs. (You probably shouldn't eat it, either.)

10-POUND DOG	20-POUND DOG	40-POUND DOG	60-POUND DOG	80-POUND DOG
2 tablespoons	¼ cup	½ cup	¾ cup	1 cup

Potato Water

My grandmother saved the water used in boiling potatoes for her gravies. I skim off a little after cooking, let it cool, and share it with our dogs. They love it. You can provide your dog with something that she'll think is a great treat, yet it has virtually no calories and is easy on the digestion.

Cook potatoes without salt, adding it instead while the potatoes are being mashed to prevent your dogs from receiving a shock of sodium. Let the potato water cool to just above room temperature and then mix in with your dog's food.

10-POUND DOG	20-POUND DOG	40-POUND DOG	60-POUND DOG	80-POUND DOG
2 teaspoons	4 teaspoons	2 tablespoons	3 tablespoons	¼ cup

Sweet Potatoes and Yams

Don't save this treat just for Thanksgiving; they're great additions to your dog's diet throughout the year. Just skip the brown sugar and marshmallows. If you prefer to include the nutritious skins, scrub well and grate the tubers for easier digestion.

10-POUND DOG	20-POUND DOG	40-POUND DOG	60-POUND DOG	80-POUND DOG
2 tablespoons	¼ cup	½ cup	¾ cup	1 cup

Tomatoes

Some chopped tomatoes added to the dog bowl provide a little fresh taste and plenty of vitamin C. When cooked, their amount of lycopene soars, which helps protect your dog's heart. As with potatoes, any green spots should be removed. If you grow your own, make sure your dog doesn't eat the green tomatoes, leaves, or stems, as these contain toxic chemicals.

10-POUND DOG	20-POUND DOG	40-POUND DOG	60-POUND DOG	80-POUND DOG
1 tablespoon	2 tablespoons	3 tablespoons	¼ cup	⅓ cup

DAIRY

Cheese

Yes, dogs love cheese, and it's hard to resist sharing. Unfortunately it's high in fat, and many adult dogs have lost their ability to process dairy products. Whether it is cheddar, Parmesan, goat cheese, or cream cheeses, if you're considering sharing some scraps with your dog, do so in moderation.

I've talked to quite a few people who use cheese in training their dogs and come to me when their dogs have diarrhea, hoping to find a solution because their dog can no longer eat their regular food. In most cases, it's the cheese used in training. When your dog is really performing well, you're going to "jackpot" your dog with a lot of treats. Cheese is such a high-value food for dogs that it's better to use it in a bonding exercise or to exploit the sticky factor in creating time-consuming snacks.

We usually clean out the cheese grater by dividing it up among the dogs, or make them all sit while taking turns licking the goat cheese wrapper. It's even more fun to feed them one string of grated cheese at a time, because it prolongs their enjoyment.

10-POUND DOG	20-POUND DOG	40-POUND DOG	60-POUND DOG	80-POUND DOG
½ teaspoon	1 teaspoon	1½ teaspoons	2 teaspoons	1 tablespoon

Eggs

Eggs are the perfect protein source, and your dog will surely love them. Sharing with your dog is also a great way to practice your omelet-making skills. Cook the dog's eggs before you cook your own to prevent any salt or pepper from getting into the eggs.

10-POUND DOG	20-POUND DOG	40-POUND DOG	60-POUND DOG	80-POUND DOG
¼ egg	½ egg	1 egg	1½ eggs	2 eggs

Yogurt

A little plain low-fat yogurt adds beneficial bacteria to help your dog's digestive system and brings zing to the breakfast bowl. Steer clear of flavored yogurt with added sugar because it adds unnecessary calories and flavorings, which might turn your dog away.

10-POUND DOG	20-POUND DOG	40-POUND DOG	60-POUND DOG	80-POUND DOG
1 teaspoon	2 teaspoons	1 tablespoon	2 tablespoons	3 tablespoons

GRAINS AND NUTS

Bread

Save white bread for feeding the birds. Whole-grain bread is a healthier choice for both you and your dog.

10-POUND DOG	20-POUND DOG	40-POUND DOG	60-POUND DOG	80-POUND DOG
¼ slice	⅓ slice	½ slice	¾ slice	1 slice

Cheerios (Whole-Grain, Plain)

This simple breakfast cereal makes a great training treat because it is low in calories and added sugar, is easily portable, and makes a nice whole-grain supplement to your dog's regular diet.

10-POUND DOG	20-POUND DOG	40-POUND DOG	60-POUND DOG	80-POUND DOG
2 tablespoons	¼ cup	½ cup	¾ cup	1 cup

Oats

Once cooked, scoop out a little of your bowl of oatmeal for your dog in the morning. Dried cranberries add a little sweetness and tang, but remember: no raisins.

10-POUND DOG	20-POUND DOG	40-POUND DOG	60-POUND DOG	80-POUND DOG
1 tablespoon	2 tablespoons	¼ cup	⅓ cup	½ cup

Peanut Butter

The snack that keeps your dog's chops smacking: peanut butter. The problem with peanut butter is that it doesn't really provide much nutrition for the high amount of fat and sodium that is being ingested. Provided sparingly, it can be a good Kong Stuffing (page 48) or an ingredient in cookies. Try the freshly ground peanut butter at your grocery store; it has better flavor, and is free of hydrogenated oils and added sugar. Or make your own by following the simple recipe on page 79.

10-POUND DOG	20-POUND DOG	40-POUND DOG	60-POUND DOG	80-POUND DOG
¼ teaspoon	½ teaspoon	1 teaspoon	2 teaspoons	1 tablespoon

Rice (Brown)

White rice is stripped of its bran and germ, which also removes some of the healthy vitamins. Try cooked brown rice for a nutty taste and a larger helping of vitamins and minerals with fewer calories.

10-POUND DOG	20-POUND DOG	40-POUND DOG	60-POUND DOG	80-POUND DOG
1 tablespoon	2 tablespoons	¼ cup	⅓ cup	½ cup

MEAT AND SEAFOOD

Bacon

Bacon is far from the perfect food for your dog; it's high in fat and extremely heavy in sodium. However, when it's frying up neither man nor beast can resist the allure. The smell of cooking bacon never fails to bring our dogs running with their noses high in the air, furiously trying to capture the scent.

If you're going to break down, you're only human (and a pretty generous one at that), but follow the RDA strictly, and break it up into 10 or more tiny pieces to prolong your dog's enjoyment. Dogs rank bacon as one of the highest-value rewards, so use a nibble as an excuse to practice your training even if it's as simple as making your dog sit before getting a piece.

10-POUND DOG	20-POUND DOG	40-POUND DOG	60-POUND DOG	80-POUND DOG
½ square inch	1 square inch	2 square inches	3 square inches	4 square inches

Broth and Stock

When we're snowshoeing, I like to take a little homemade broth with us for the dogs in a Thermos. It warms them up and is a nice reward after a cold day in the snow. Broth shared with your dogs should not include onions in the preparation. See the broth recipes on pages 65 to 67, which are great for use both in your cooking and in your dog's bowl.

10-POUND DOG	20-POUND DOG	40-POUND DOG	60-POUND DOG	80-POUND DOG
⅓ cup	½ cup	⅔ cup	¾ cup	1 cup

Sardines

Most dogs enjoy the taste of fish, and this is a great snack that provides a healthy dose of omega-3 fatty acids to nourish your dog's coat and skin. You can use drained sardines that were packed in oil or water, or even sardines packed in tomato sauce to add a lycopene kick.

10-POUND DOG	20-POUND DOG	40-POUND DOG	60-POUND DOG	80-POUND DOG
¼ sardine	½ sardine	1 sardine	1½ sardines	2 sardines

SCRAMBLED EGG

The simplest thing you can do to feed your best friend better is to give your dog an egg when you're making your own breakfast. Your dog will go bonkers for this incredible food, plus it's inexpensive and easy to prepare.

Eggs are nutritionally dense; for the number of calories (75 per large egg) they provide a good amount of nutrition, especially protein, selenium, and choline. In fact, eggs have the highest biological value, meaning they are the best source of the proteins that are essential for growth and maintenance and are easily absorbed by the body.

Eggs should be cooked because the uncooked egg white prevents biotin (a B vitamin) from being absorbed, and biotin is essential for cell growth, metabolizing fats and protein, and the quality of your dog's coat.

Cooking an egg is simple in the microwave, it takes only one or two minutes, and there are only two ingredients. Don't add any butter, salt, or pepper to your dog's egg—your dog doesn't need them.

Nonstick cooking spray	Spray a microwave-safe bowl with cooking spray.
1 large egg	Add the egg and water to the bowl, then mix with a fork until fully blended.
2 tablespoons water	
	Microwave for 1 minute and 15 seconds on high. (For 2 eggs, cook for 2 minutes.)
	Allow the egg to cool to room temperature before serving.
	One egg replaces ⅓ cup of dry food, you can replace up to half of your dog's normal meal with eggs.

Sweet Potato Fries for Sharing

Even dogs reticent with vegetables will love this treat. Finish with a little salt and pepper on your portion and you'll enjoy these too. This recipe also works well with yams, parsnips, and turnips.

Preheat the oven to 425°F.

1 medium sweet potato

Peel the sweet potato and cut into strips ¼ inch square by 4 inches long.

2 tablespoons olive oil

½ teaspoon dried oregano

Combine the sweet potatoes, olive oil, and oregano on a baking sheet and toss until the potatoes are well coated.

Spread out evenly on the baking sheet, positioning the fries so they are parallel. (This will pay off when you need to flip them.) Bake for 15 minutes.

Flip the fries and bake for another 15 minutes.

Allow the fries to cool before serving (but grab your share and sprinkle with a little coarse salt while they are hot).

Yield: 2 cups

ALLOWANCE PER DAY				
10-POUND DOG	**20-POUND DOG**	**40-POUND DOG**	**60-POUND DOG**	**80-POUND DOG**
1 fry	2 fries	4 fries	6 fries	8 fries

Your best friend is a foodie.

SALMON PATTIES

"Fish, for me?" Your dog will look at you in amazement after the first bite. Although your dog is thinking it's just a treat, it's really a snack that provides protein, vitamin D, selenium, and a nice helping of omega-3 fatty acids. Try these yourself hot off the griddle or cold over a crisp salad (see Note).

Panko bread crumbs are commonly used in Japanese cooking to provide a crunchy crust with five simple ingredients: flour, sugar, yeast, oil, and salt. This is a healthier choice than other manufactured bread crumbs because panko is made without high-fructose corn syrup, hydrogenated oils, and other added sugars.

1 (14.5-ounce) can salmon	Empty the canned salmon (with juices) into a medium bowl. Flake with a fork to separate and remove any bones.
2 large eggs 1¼ cups panko bread crumbs ⅓ cup minced fresh parsley	Add the eggs, bread crumbs, and parsley and stir until well combined. Form patties by packing the mixture into a ½-cup measuring cup and tapping gently into the palm of your hand. Press lightly into a 3½-inch patty.
2 tablespoons olive oil	Heat the oil over medium heat and cook the salmon patties for 4 to 5 minutes per side, until they are nicely browned. After the patties have cooled slightly, break up and serve! Store in the refrigerator for up to 4 days or in the freezer for up to 3 weeks.
	YIELD: 6 patties

NOTE: If you would like to make the same recipe for yourself, add the following to the salmon mixture: ⅓ cup minced onion, plus salt and pepper as desired. However, be sure to set aside your dog's portion first to prevent your dog from getting the onion-laced bits. (Use your dog's portion to test the oil and cooking time.)

ALLOWANCE PER DAY				
10-POUND DOG ¼ patty	**20-POUND DOG** ⅓ patty	**40-POUND DOG** ⅔ patty	**60-POUND DOG** ¾ patty	**80-POUND DOG** 1 patty

DUTCH BABY PANCAKE

When I was a kid, this was one of our favorite breakfast treats. My mom would top it with a squeeze of lemon and confectioners' sugar for us. Adding sliced fresh strawberries makes it even more delicious. For your dog, though, serve it plain: The crunchy edges and the puffy egg base are a treat in both texture and taste all by themselves.

Preheat the oven to 400°F. Place an 8-inch cast-iron skillet in the oven and heat it for about 5 minutes.

½ cup all-purpose flour

½ cup 2% milk

3 large eggs

¼ teaspoon salt

Combine the flour, milk, eggs, and salt in a blender and mix at medium speed for 30 seconds.

¼ cup unsalted butter

Melt the butter in the preheated skillet, and then pour in the egg mixture.

Return the skillet to the oven and cook the pancake for 12 to 15 minutes.

Serve immediately to humans, but wait a few minutes for it to cool off for your canine pal.

YIELD: 1 pancake will serve 2 people

ALLOWANCE PER DAY				
10-POUND DOG	**20-POUND DOG**	**40-POUND DOG**	**60-POUND DOG**	**80-POUND DOG**
1 square inch	2 square inches	3 square inches	4 square inches	6 square inches

BAKED APPLES

Winter is a good time for this recipe because it's easy to prepare from ingredients that are on hand and comforting on long, dark nights. When sharing this treat with your best friend, be sure to let it cool to slightly above room temperature before you serve it.

Preheat the oven to 350°F.

4 red apples (Braeburn or Red Rome are good choices)

If desired, peel the apples with a vegetable peeler.

Using a melon baller, scoop out the stem, core, and seeds of the apples, leaving about ½ inch of the bottom intact.

Arrange the apples in a pie dish or an 8-inch square baking dish.

¼ cup firmly packed brown sugar

1 teaspoon ground cinnamon

½ teaspoon ground ginger

½ cup unsweetened apple juice

Mix the brown sugar, cinnamon, and ginger in a small bowl.

Stuff each apple with 2 tablespoons of the sugar mixture.

Pour the apple juice over and around the apples.

4 teaspoons unsalted butter

Dot each apple with 1 teaspoon of the butter.

Bake for 1 hour, or until the apples are puffed and tender.

Greek yogurt, for topping (optional)

Serve with 2 tablespoons yogurt per apple, if desired.

YIELD: 4 apples

ALLOWANCE PER DAY				
10-POUND DOG	**20-POUND DOG**	**40-POUND DOG**	**60-POUND DOG**	**80-POUND DOG**
⅛ apple	¼ apple	⅓ apple	½ apple	⅔ apple

BLUEBERRY PANCAKES

Ever since Jackson stole half a blueberry pie off the counter, he loved blueberries. Sunday morning at our house is blueberry pancake day, and the sight of the griddle brings all the dogs around. The secret to blueberry pancakes that are not streaked with blue (not that the dogs care) is to add the blueberries just after the batter has been set on the griddle. This recipe makes a thicker pancake, but you can make thinner pancakes by adding a tablespoon or two of milk to the batter.

🐾 Heat a griddle or frying pan over medium heat. You'll know when the griddle is ready when a few drops of water bubble and dance across the surface of the grill.

1 cup all-purpose flour

1 tablespoon sugar

½ teaspoon salt

½ teaspoon baking powder

¼ teaspoon baking soda

🐾 Whisk together the flour, sugar, salt, baking powder, and baking soda in a medium bowl. Create a well in the center of the bowl.

2 large eggs

1 cup plain low-fat yogurt

2 tablespoons unsalted butter, melted, plus more for the griddle

🐾 Add the eggs, yogurt, and melted butter to the center of the well and blend with a fork. Fold the egg mixture into the dry ingredients until combined thoroughly. Do not overmix.

Grease the griddle, and pour the batter onto the griddle using a ¼-cup measuring cup.

1 cup fresh or thawed frozen blueberries

🐾 Cover the surface of each pancake with 10 to 12 blueberries.

Cook for 4 to 5 minutes, until bubbles start to appear on the top, and then flip and cook for 4 to 5 minutes longer.

Place the finished pancakes in an oven heated to 200°F to keep warm until all the pancakes are cooked.

🐾 **YIELD:** 8 pancakes

ALLOWANCE PER DAY				
10-POUND DOG	**20-POUND DOG**	**40-POUND DOG**	**60-POUND DOG**	**80-POUND DOG**
⅓ pancake	½ pancake	⅔ pancake	¾ pancake	1 pancake

KEBABS FOR DOGS

When you're having a summer barbecue, don't forget your best friend who spent the better part of the day retrieving your Frisbee. Grilled meat has a special appeal for dogs, and it's worth putting aside a few pieces of chicken and vegetables to share. Just remember to remove the skewers before serving!

¼ cup boneless, skinless chicken thighs, cut into 1-inch cubes

2 tablespoons olive oil

Sprinkle of garlic powder (less than ⅛ teaspoon)

1 teaspoon minced fresh thyme, rosemary, or oregano

¼ cup chopped vegetables or fruit, such as red bell peppers, zucchini, apples, pears, or peaches

Place the chicken cubes, olive oil, garlic powder, and the herb of your choice in a small bowl and toss to coat thoroughly.

Refrigerate for at least 30 minutes and up to 24 hours.

Soak your (wooden) skewers in water to cover for about 30 minutes before cooking.

Heat the grill to medium-low, a temperature in which you can hold your hand for 5 seconds 5 inches above the surface of the grill.

Thread alternating pieces of chicken, vegetables, and fruit on each skewer. Brush a little of the marinade over the vegetables, then discard the excess marinade.

Grill, turning each kebab one-quarter turn every 2 minutes. Cook the last side for a total of 3 minutes, so that the skewers have cooked for a total of 9 minutes.

Allow the chicken and vegetables to cool to room temperature, then remove the skewers and serve.

YIELD: ½ cup

ALLOWANCE PER DAY

As an occasional meal, replace cup for cup of your dog's regular meal.

Your best friend found love at the shelter.

TUNA SANDWICH LEFTOVERS

When you're making a tuna fish sandwich, what's the first thing you do? You drain off the water and pour it down the sink. Next you grab two pieces of bread, being careful to avoid the heel of the loaf. Put these two things you weren't even going to use together and you have a nice little pick-me-up for your pooch.

1 slice whole-grain bread

1 (6-ounce) can tuna, packed in water

Place the bread in a small bowl.

Drain the tuna water over the bread and let sit for 3 minutes to allow all the liquid to be absorbed.

Add 1 tablespoon of the tuna, blend with a fork, and serve.

YIELD: 1 slice; store extra in the refrigerator for up to 3 days

ALLOWANCE PER DAY				
10-POUND DOG	**20-POUND DOG**	**40-POUND DOG**	**60-POUND DOG**	**80-POUND DOG**
⅓ slice	½ slice	⅔ slice	¾ slice	1 slice

CHEESE CHIPS

Sure, these cheese chips are great rolled up while slightly warm and then stuffed into a Kong toy. However, they are also a nice addition to your own salad and make a nice garnish when you're having guests.

2 tablespoons freshly grated
Parmesan cheese

In a small nonstick skillet, spread the cheese thinly and evenly in the pan to form a circle using the appropriate amount for your dog (see below). Repeat with the remaining cheese to form more circles.

Put the pan over medium heat for 2 to 3 minutes, until the cheese is bubbling and slightly browned.

Remove the pan from the heat and allow the chips to cool in the pan for 5 to 6 minutes. Blot lightly with a paper towel to remove excess grease. While warm, the chips can be rolled and inserted into a Kong toy.

Reserve leftover chips at room temperature in an airtight container for up to 2 days.

YIELD: 2 to 6 chips, depending on your dog

ALLOWANCE PER DAY				
10-POUND DOG	**20-POUND DOG**	**40-POUND DOG**	**60-POUND DOG**	**80-POUND DOG**
½ teaspoon cheese	1 teaspoon cheese	1½ teaspoons cheese	2 teaspoons cheese	1 tablespoon cheese

TREATS

KONG STUFFINGS

ROBERT'S LIVER TREATS

LOYALTY LIVER PÂTÉ

PUMPKIN PUPPY PUFFS

SARDINE CROUTONS

SEA BISCUITS

RICE REBORN

PUMPKIN ICE CREAM

PEANUT BUTTER AND BANANA ICE CREAM

WONTON, MEET PARMESAN

LIVER BROWNIES

DOGS ♥ JERKY

GOOD GIRL GIZZARDS

DUCK HEARTS

BEEF STOCK

CHICKEN STOCK

FISH STOCK

PUPPY PESTO

GIBLET GRAVY

PUMPKIN PUREE

PUMPKIN SEEDS

The quickest way to a man's heart might be through his stomach, but since dogs are wired differently, the message goes right to the brain. Training can become much more effective with a little morsel in your hand. The size of the treat doesn't matter as much as the reward of a treat itself. Try using healthy items like Cheerios (page 33), the recipe for Good Girl Gizzards (page 63), or even pieces of safe, pitted and cored fruits (page 29) instead of cheese or hot dogs, which are both high in fat and sodium.

Treats can also be used to provide a little energy boost or to keep your dog busy. Leaving a mischievous dog at home when you go to work? Try stuffing a Kong, a hard rubber toy designed to hold treats, with something that will keep your dog busy. Kongs not only get your dog chewing, which helps maintain dental hygiene, they also make your dog work to get the treat out, so they act as great mental stimulation. Most damage in your home occurs shortly after you leave, so if you can keep a dog occupied both physically and mentally, a dog will have less energy to spend making trouble.

If you don't like the idea of feeding your dog raw bones as treats, or it's the middle of winter and not the best time to set your dog in the yard for a gnawing session with a messy bone, consider giving your dog a stuffed Kong to keep her mentally stimulated and occupied with a fun game.

As your dog's talent for treat extraction develops, increase the difficulty; freeze the food the night before, or put the filled Kong in a clean sock. If your dog becomes proficient at getting the Kong out of the sock, try tying the sock in a knot. This also has a great benefit of "brushing" your dog's teeth while working the knot out. Dogs should be monitored with this sock "puzzle," however, and this should not be done with dogs who are known to swallow inappropriate objects.

KONG STUFFINGS

Cheddar cheese melted in the microwave bubbles up and sticks to the sides of a Kong, really making your dog work to get it out. A great way to make a little bit of food stretch your dog's enjoyment is to stuff a few strands of cheese in a Kong and melt it in the microwave at high heat for 15 seconds. Allow the Kong to cool in the microwave for at least 3 minutes; otherwise, the cheese tends to drip out and/or your dog might burn himself while devouring this treat.

Cream cheese is useful for hiding pills, and even better if it's fat free. Cream cheese has great sticking power inside a Kong, giving your dog a real challenge. You can make the cream cheese easier to smear by mixing in a few drops of hot water.

Freeze unsweetened applesauce inside a Kong for a delicious, low-calorie cooldown treat. Plug the open end with another dog treat or a scrap of bread first, then add the applesauce, to prevent any spills in the freezer.

Cottage cheese and rice is often suggested as a gentle meal for dogs with sensitive stomachs, and it can be frozen in a Kong as another summertime treat.

Peanut butter and plain Cheerios mixed together provides a sticky and crunchy teaser; follow the suggested amounts in the "Foods Worth Sharing" section (page 28).

Yogurt mixed with a high-quality dry dog food makes breakfast last longer and provides probiotics to help your dog's digestive system.

ROBERT'S LIVER TREATS

My friend Robert gave me this recipe that he used in training his Welsh Corgis. These treats drive our dogs bonkers, but they quickly settle down and wait patiently to be the first in line. For an effective training reward these can't be beat, but let's be honest: beef liver stinks. I prefer making them in the summer, when windows and doors can be opened to air out the kitchen. If you have a gas grill with a burner, you can also experiment with making these outdoors!

5 cups water	Bring the water to a boil in a large stockpot.
1 pound beef liver, sliced ¼ inch thick (ask your butcher to do this for you)	Add the beef liver and return to a boil.
	Decrease the heat to a simmer and cook for an additional 10 minutes.
	Drain the liver and set aside to cool. Save the broth for any recipes in this book calling for stock, or to pour over dog food.
	Preheat the oven to 275°F.
Nonstick cooking spray	Spray a 9 by 13-inch baking sheet with nonstick cooking spray.
1 tablespoon garlic powder	Cut the liver into 1-inch squares and toss with the garlic powder on the baking sheet.
	Bake for 2 hours. Turn off the oven and allow the liver to cool on the baking sheet in the closed oven.
	After the treats have cooled, store in an airtight container for up to 2 weeks or in the freezer for up to 6 months.

YIELD: 2 cups treats, 4½ cups stock

ALLOWANCE PER DAY				
10-POUND DOG	**20-POUND DOG**	**40-POUND DOG**	**60-POUND DOG**	**80-POUND DOG**
½ teaspoon	1 teaspoon	1½ teaspoons	2 teaspoons	1 tablespoon

Your best friend is a bed hog.

LOYALTY LIVER PÂTÉ

When I make this, the dogs finish it up and then follow me around for the rest of the day, wondering if there'll be a second helping. There will be more, but since liver is so rich, I space out the servings to every three or four days.

Just a bit smeared inside a Kong toy will keep your dog busy and mentally stimulated. If your dog is new to the joys of having a snack inside a Kong, this is an irresistible treat for getting started. If your dog hasn't had liver before, start out using small amounts and see how your dog tolerates it.

1 slice bacon

In a large skillet, cook the bacon over medium heat for 5 minutes, or until crisp. Remove the bacon from the skillet, reserving 1 tablespoon of drippings. Drain and crumble the bacon; set aside.

½ pound chicken livers

⅛ teaspoon garlic powder

Add the chicken livers and garlic powder to the reserved drippings. Cook over medium-high heat for 5 minutes, stirring occasionally.

¼ teaspoon dried thyme

¼ cup plain low-fat yogurt

Add the thyme and cook for an additional 3 minutes, or until the livers have browned nicely on the outside.

Remove the livers from the heat and let cool to room temperature.

⅔ cup panko bread crumbs

Combine the reserved bacon, livers, yogurt, and bread crumbs in a food processor and process for 15 seconds. Scrape down the sides of the bowl and process for another 10 seconds, until smooth.

Store in the refrigerator for up to 1 week, or spoon into ice cube trays, freeze, and then transfer the frozen cubes to a plastic bag and store frozen for up to 2 months.

YIELD: 1⅓ cups

ALLOWANCE PER DAY				
10-POUND DOG	**20-POUND DOG**	**40-POUND DOG**	**60-POUND DOG**	**80-POUND DOG**
½ teaspoon	1 teaspoon	1½ teaspoons	2 teaspoons	1 tablespoon

PUMPKIN PUPPY PUFFS

Light and fluffy, these are a great treat for stuffing into a Kong. If you'd like to give them as gifts or just speed up the process, you can use a pastry bag with a decorative tip.

If using homemade pumpkin puree, prior to adding the pumpkin into the other ingredients, set it in a fine-mesh strainer for 5 minutes to allow some of the liquid to drain off.

	Preheat the oven to 350°F.
1 large egg	Beat the egg in a medium bowl.
⅔ cup cream of wheat or cream of rice cereal	Add all of the remaining ingredients and stir until well blended.
¼ cup nonfat instant powdered milk	
1 cup canned solid-pack pumpkin puree or homemade puree (page 71)	
1 tablespoon canola oil	
½ teaspoon ground cinnamon	
Nonstick cooking spray	Drop the batter in 1-teaspoon amounts onto a lightly greased baking sheet about ½ inch apart.
	Bake until lightly browned, 20 minutes for a soft and chewy treat or 25 to 28 minutes for a crunchier treat.
	Store in the refrigerator for up to 2 weeks or the freezer for up to 2 months.

YIELD: 50 treats

ALLOWANCE PER DAY				
10-POUND DOG	**20-POUND DOG**	**40-POUND DOG**	**60-POUND DOG**	**80-POUND DOG**
2 treats	3 treats	5 treats	7 treats	9 treats

SARDINE CROUTONS

Cutting the croutons ¼ inch larger than the hole in the Kong will help hold the croutons inside and give your dog something to work at.

1 water-packed sardine 🐾 Mash the sardine with a fork in a small bowl until the fish is reduced to a paste. Remove any visible bones.

1 slice whole-wheat bread 🐾 Toast the bread until lightly browned.

Cut the bread into ½- to 1-inch cubes, depending on the size of the Kong opening.

Add the bread cubes to the mashed sardine, and mix well to coat the bread.

Refrigerate any unused portion for up to 3 days.

ALLOWANCE PER DAY				
10-POUND DOG	**20-POUND DOG**	**40-POUND DOG**	**60-POUND DOG**	**80-POUND DOG**
¼ slice bread	½ slice bread	⅔ slice bread	¾ slice bread	1 slice bread

SEA BISCUITS

A serving of fish is just the thing for Labradors or other water breeds. The oils in the fish go right to improving the quality of coat and skin. The soft nature of this treat makes it easy for you to put it into a Kong and easier for your dog to get it out.

Preheat the oven to 350°F.

2 large eggs

1 tablespoon dried kelp

Whisk the eggs and kelp in a medium bowl until blended.

2 (5 ounce) cans oil-packed tuna, drained

2 cups panko bread crumbs

Add the tuna and bread crumbs, and stir until thoroughly combined.

Nonstick cooking spray

Spray an 8-inch square baking dish with nonstick cooking spray and press the mixture into the dish.

With a knife, cut all the way through the biscuits in four lines in each direction, approximately 1½ inches apart, to make 25 treats.

Bake for 15 minutes, or until lightly browned. Allow the biscuits to cool, and then tear them apart at the score lines to make individual treats.

Store in the refrigerator for up to 1 week or in the freezer for up to 2 months.

YIELD: 25 treats

ALLOWANCE PER DAY				
10-POUND DOG	**20-POUND DOG**	**40-POUND DOG**	**60-POUND DOG**	**80-POUND DOG**
1 biscuit	2 biscuits	3 biscuits	4 biscuits	5 biscuits

Your best friend shakes on it.

RICE REBORN

Rather than let extra rice go to waste, transform it into a casserole for your dog. Softening the rice with water makes this dish easy to digest, and the cheese helps to disguise the fact that healthy vegetables are inside. This makes an excellent Kong stuffing or it can be used to hide medicine.

Preheat the oven to 350°F.

Nonstick cooking spray — Spray an 8-inch square casserole dish with cooking spray.

2 large eggs — In a medium bowl, beat the eggs with the parsley.
¼ cup chopped fresh parsley

1 cup cooked rice — Add the rice, vegetables, water, and cheese and mix until well blended.

½ cup finely chopped or grated carrots, broccoli, or green beans

Pour the mixture into the prepared dish and bake for 25 minutes, or until all the liquid is absorbed and the top is lightly browned.

¼ cup water

¼ cup grated cheddar cheese

Store in the refrigerator for up to 4 days or in the freezer for up to 1 month.

YIELD: 3 cups

ALLOWANCE PER DAY				
10-POUND DOG	**20-POUND DOG**	**40-POUND DOG**	**60-POUND DOG**	**80-POUND DOG**
¼ cup	⅓ cup	½ cup	¾ cup	1 cup

PUMPKIN ICE CREAM

Did you know that dogs don't sweat? It's the panting that helps them cool their head and to some extent their body. To help your dog keep cool, try ice cream. This is a treat best served outdoors, as it can be kind of messy if your dog noses it across the floor while licking away. It's also a great treat for stuffing in a Kong.

Chopped-up dog cookies or other treats like Good Girl Gizzards (page 63) can also be mixed in if you don't have chicken livers on hand.

For older dogs with sensitive mouths, allow the frozen cubes to thaw for a few minutes before feeding.

1 cup water

Bring the water and chicken livers to a boil in a small saucepan; decrease the heat and simmer for 8 minutes.

2 chicken livers

Drain the livers and reserve the stock for pouring over food or for making dog cookies. Allow the livers to cool, and then chop finely.

1 cup plain low-fat yogurt

1 cup solid-pack pumpkin puree

Combine the livers, yogurt, and pumpkin in a medium bowl and stir until smooth.

Spoon the mixture into an ice cube tray and freeze for 4 to 6 hours.

YIELD: 12 ice-cream cubes, ¾ cup stock

ALLOWANCE PER DAY				
10-POUND DOG	**20-POUND DOG**	**40-POUND DOG**	**60-POUND DOG**	**80-POUND DOG**
1 cube	2 cubes	3 cubes	4 cubes	5 cubes

PEANUT BUTTER AND BANANA ICE CREAM

This recipe offers another delicious way to keep cool. The molasses is included not only to sweeten the ice cream a bit but also to provide important nutrients like calcium, iron, magnesium, and potassium. Be sure to buy blackstrap molasses to ensure that it contains the important vitamins and minerals; other forms of molasses are mostly just sugars.

The peanut butter in this ice cream increases the fat content, so it's higher in calories. Please note the reduced feeding amounts.

For older dogs with sensitive mouths, allow the frozen cubes to thaw for a few minutes before feeding.

½ ripe banana

1 cup plain low-fat yogurt

2 tablespoons peanut butter (natural style preferred)

2 tablespoons blackstrap molasses

Mash the banana well in a medium bowl. Add all of the remaining ingredients and stir until smooth.

Spoon the mixture into an ice cube tray and freeze for 4 to 6 hours.

YIELD: 12 ice-cream cubes

ALLOWANCE PER DAY				
10-POUND DOG	**20-POUND DOG**	**40-POUND DOG**	**60-POUND DOG**	**80-POUND DOG**
1 cube	1 cube	2 cubes	3 cubes	4 cubes

WONTON, MEET PARMESAN

Here's a little Asian–Italian fusion for your dog. The beauty of wonton wrappers is that they have no desire to be the star of the show. In Asian restaurants, wonton wrappers are used to deliver tasty fillings and dip into both sweet and savory sauces. They stay in the background in this recipe as well, letting the true star— a tiny bit of Parmesan cheese—take center stage. If you'd like to add even more of a twist, cut each wonton wrapper into four lengthwise strips, cover with the toppings, and then twist lightly before baking.

Preheat the oven to 400°F.

Nonstick cooking spray

Coat a baking sheet with cooking spray.

12 wonton wrappers

Arrange the wonton wrappers on the baking sheet in a single layer, edge to edge.

1 egg white, beaten with 1 teaspoon water

Brush each wrapper with the beaten egg white, then sprinkle evenly with the oregano and cheese.

½ teaspoon dried oregano leaves, crumbled

Cut each wonton wrapper twice diagonally using a knife or pizza cutter in an "X" motion, creating 4 triangles.

¼ cup freshly grated Parmesan cheese

Bake for 6 to 7 minutes, until the edges are brown.

Transfer to a cooling rack to cool completely.

Store in an airtight container at room temperature for up to 3 days or in the freezer for up to 1 month.

YIELD: 48 treats

ALLOWANCE PER DAY				
10-POUND DOG	**20-POUND DOG**	**40-POUND DOG**	**60-POUND DOG**	**80-POUND DOG**
2 treats	4 treats	7 treats	9 treats	12 treats

Your best friend shares your dreams.

LIVER BROWNIES

Who doesn't love a good brownie? There's no reason to leave your dog out of the brownie fun: Simply substitute liver for chocolate. This makes a soft, dense brownie that is excellent for stuffing inside a Kong. Your dog will want you to choose beef liver because dogs love it, but chicken livers work just as well and don't have such a heavy scent.

Because liver is high in vitamin A, share this treat sparingly. It freezes well for up to 3 months, so store some away as a special treat.

	Preheat the oven to 350°F.
Nonstick cooking spray	Apply a generous amount of cooking spray to an 8-inch square baking dish.
1 cup quick-cooking rolled oats	Pulse the oatmeal in a food processor until it is a fine texture.
1 teaspoon garlic powder **3 large eggs** **¼ pound liver (beef or chicken)**	Add the garlic powder, eggs, and liver to the food processor and blend for 30 seconds.
2 cups seven-grain cereal (look for it next to the oatmeal)	Add the cereal 1 cup at a time and pulse until blended
	Pour the batter into the prepared baking dish and bake for 25 minutes. (Immediately rinse the food processor to prevent any remaining liver from sticking.)
	Allow the brownies to cool to room temperature, then cut at 1-inch intervals in both directions.
	Store in the refrigerator for up to 1 week or in the freezer for up to 3 months.
	YIELD: 64 brownies

ALLOWANCE PER DAY (MAXIMUM 2 OR 3 TIMES PER WEEK)				
10-POUND DOG	**20-POUND DOG**	**40-POUND DOG**	**60-POUND DOG**	**80-POUND DOG**
½ square inch	1 square inch	1½ square inches	2 square inches	3 square inches

DOGS ♥ JERKY

My mom assisted me each week in the Dog Stew kitchen and came up with this recipe on her own. You can also substitute boneless, skinless chicken breasts for the beef heart. The molasses provides sweetness to the jerky and the anise adds a delightful scent that dogs will appreciate.

🐾 Preheat the oven to 275°F.

Nonstick cooking spray 🐾 Apply a generous amount of cooking spray to a baking sheet.

1 pound beef heart 🐾 Trim all fat from the beef heart. Bring the water and beef to a boil in a 2-quart saucepan. Decrease the heat to medium-low and simmer for 20 minutes.

6 cups water

Drain the beef, reserving the broth for use in other recipes. Allow the beef to cool, then slice into strips ¼ inch thick, cutting in the direction of the meat's grain to make the meat even chewier.

2 tablespoons blackstrap molasses 🐾 Whisk together the molasses, apple cider vinegar, and anise powder, if using, in a medium bowl.

2 tablespoons apple cider vinegar (with the "mother," page 13) Add the sliced beef to the molasses mixture and stir to coat evenly.

½ teaspoon ground star anise powder (optional) Place the beef strips on the baking sheet, slightly separated, and bake for 1 hour, or until dry.

Store at room temperature for up to 1 week or in the freezer for up to 1 month.

🐾 **YIELD:** about 2 cups

ALLOWANCE PER DAY				
10-POUND DOG	**20-POUND DOG**	**40-POUND DOG**	**60-POUND DOG**	**80-POUND DOG**
1 strip	2 strips	3 strips	4 strips	5 strips

GOOD GIRL GIZZARDS

Sure, they're small. But pulling these out for dog training makes your dog as happy as you used to be when somebody offered you a piece of candy as a child. The joy is the same even if the treat is not.

Try this small batch to start. Next time, you may want to make double or triple the batch size. It's barely any effort, and your dog will definitely deserve more as your training progresses.

5 cups water	Bring the water to a boil in a 2-quart saucepan.
1 pound chicken gizzards	Add the gizzards and return the water to a boil, uncovered. Decrease the heat to low and simmer for 20 minutes, uncovered.
	Drain the gizzards and allow them to cool enough to handle. Reserve and freeze the stock for use in any recipe in this book calling for chicken stock.
	Preheat the oven to 300°F.
	Cut the gizzards into ¼-inch slices.
1 tablespoon olive oil	Toss the gizzards with the olive oil and garlic powder on a large rimmed baking sheet.
¼ teaspoon garlic powder	Bake for 1 hour, tossing 2 to 3 times.
	Turn off the oven and dry the gizzards in the oven for 1 hour.
	Store in the refrigerator for up to 3 weeks or in the freezer for up to 3 months.
	YIELD: 1 cup

ALLOWANCE PER DAY				
10-POUND DOG	**20-POUND DOG**	**40-POUND DOG**	**60-POUND DOG**	**80-POUND DOG**
1 teaspoon	2 teaspoons	1 tablespoon	2 tablespoons	3 tablespoons

DUCK HEARTS

Many dogs on restricted diets due to possible allergies are often prescribed a duck and potato diet. Duck is a novel protein source that most dogs have not been exposed to earlier in life, and they are therefore less likely to have an allergic reaction to it. If your dog has allergy concerns, you should also limit the protein sources in treats. Although this recipe was created for dogs with allergies, it's a great treat for any dog. I bake them longer, until they're dried and crunchy, and dogs love them. The softer version provides a great place to hide medicine.

Duck hearts are often available at Asian grocery stores, but if you can't find them you can always substitute chicken hearts, as long as your dog does not have any allergy concerns.

Two batches fit well on an 11 by 14-inch baking sheet if you would like to double the recipe.

Preheat the oven to 325°F.

1 pound duck hearts

1 tablespoon canola oil

1 tablespoon dried rosemary, crumbled

½ teaspoon garlic powder

Mix all of the ingredients together in a medium bowl.

Spread on a rimmed baking sheet and bake for 45 minutes to achieve a soft browned treat perfect for senior dogs. Or cook for a total of 1 hour 15 minutes, until crunchy and dry, to prolong their shelf life. Toss every 30 minutes to ensure even cooking.

Store soft treats for up to 1 week in the refrigerator or up to 2 months in the freezer. Store crunchy treats for up to 1 month in the refrigerator or up to 6 months in the freezer.

YIELD: 80 treats

ALLOWANCE PER DAY				
10-POUND DOG	**20-POUND DOG**	**40-POUND DOG**	**60-POUND DOG**	**80-POUND DOG**
2 pieces	3 pieces	5 pieces	6 pieces	8 pieces

Beef Stock

If we took a poll based on the number of wagging tails, beef would probably come up as the number-one favorite canine flavor. This stock is incredibly easy to prepare, and using beef neck bones is an inexpensive choice that also utilizes a secondary cut of meat left over from human food production. If your local grocery store doesn't carry neck bones, try to find an Asian grocery store, where you can usually find these bones for just a couple of dollars.

While you're waiting for the stock to cool, grab a leash and the garbage, and then head out for a walk after stopping at the trash can. By immediately taking out the trash, you can prevent curious noses from instigating a garbage party and ingesting dangerous pieces of bone.

Preheat the oven to 400°F.

2 pounds beef neck bones

¼ teaspoon garlic powder

Sprinkle the bones with the garlic powder and roast the bones for 15 minutes in a baking dish or rimmed baking sheet.

Turn the bones over and roast for another 20 minutes, until the bones are browned. The meat on the bones will not yet be fully cooked through.

6 cups water

While the bones are roasting, bring the water to a boil in a large stockpot over high heat.

1 medium carrot, coarsely chopped

Add the roasted bones, carrot, and tomato to the boiling water. Replace the lid and allow the water to return to a boil for 5 minutes.

1 Roma tomato, sliced into quarters

Decrease the heat to low and simmer with the lid on for 1 hour. The stock will be pretty good at this point. If you simmer the stock for 2 hours, it will be even richer tasting and you'll be tempted to use the stock in your own cooking.

Strain the stock. The small amount of meat can be removed from the bones and shared over dinner for an extra-special treat. Discard bones and vegetables.

The stock and meat can be refrigerated for up to 4 days or frozen for up to 6 months.

YIELD: about 5 cups of stock and 2 cups of meat from the bones

BEEF STOCK ALLOWANCE PER DAY				
10-POUND DOG	**20-POUND DOG**	**40-POUND DOG**	**60-POUND DOG**	**80-POUND DOG**
¼ cup	⅓ cup	½ cup	⅔ cup	1 cup

MEAT FROM BONES ALLOWANCE PER DAY				
10-POUND DOG	**20-POUND DOG**	**40-POUND DOG**	**60-POUND DOG**	**80-POUND DOG**
1 tablespoon	2 tablespoons	3 tablespoons	⅓ cup	½ cup

CHICKEN STOCK

When making this stock for the dogs, you can pack it with flavors and use it as an excuse to clean out the fridge a bit. If you have saved other fruits and vegetables that are still fresh but not likely to be used in the next couple of days, go ahead and add a cup or two. Don't worry so much about precision—you never have to make the same stock twice because you may not be stocking the same ingredients in the fridge.

The resulting stock will be rich with flavor, vitamins, and minerals and can be used to moisten dry food or in any of the cookie recipes.

10 cups water

Bones from 1 chicken carcass, all skin removed (see Note)

2 medium carrots, chopped

2 stalks celery, chopped

1 apple, cored and chopped

1 cup packed fresh spinach

1 teaspoon dried rosemary

1 teaspoon dried basil

¼ teaspoon garlic powder

Bring the water to a boil in a large stockpot over high heat.

Add the chicken bones, carrots, celery, apple, spinach, rosemary, basil, and garlic powder and bring to a boil. Skim any foam from the top of the water with a spoon.

Decrease the heat to low and simmer with the lid on for 40 minutes.

Strain the stock and discard the bones and vegetables.

The stock can be refrigerated for up to 1 week or frozen for up to 6 months.

YIELD: about 9 cups

NOTE: To create a richer-tasting broth that you can use in your own meals as well, first preheat the oven to 400°F and then roast the chicken bones for 15 to 20 minutes, until they turn a rich golden brown. Proceed as directed.

ALLOWANCE PER DAY				
10-POUND DOG	**20-POUND DOG**	**40-POUND DOG**	**60-POUND DOG**	**80-POUND DOG**
¼ cup	⅓ cup	½ cup	⅔ cup	1 cup

FISH STOCK

Most of the cookie recipes in this cookbook call for chicken or beef stock, but you can easily substitute fish stock to make treats even more tempting. Occasionally, we buy a whole salmon and combine the backbone and parts that were mangled in the filleting process with a few cups of water, and 20 minutes later we have a rich-tasting fish stock. Nothing else is needed because the fish will tell the tale on its own. I love to give the dogs a little freshly made and cooled broth as a post-walk treat. Mackerel, halibut, and orange roughy are also good choices. If you're feeling ambitious, go ahead and pick the fish off the bones after making the stock, and serve that as an extra-special treat over the evening's dinner.

Fish (anything you can spare, such as heads, backbones, or scraps)

Water

Bring the fish and enough water to cover by 1 inch to a boil in a large stockpot over high heat.

Decrease the heat to a simmer and cook for 20 minutes.

Remove from the heat and allow the stock to cool.

Strain, cool, and give a bit to your dog while it's fresh.

Store in the refrigerator for up to 1 week or in the freezer for up to 2 months.

YIELD: this will depend on how much fish and water you add to the pot

ALLOWANCE PER DAY				
10-POUND DOG	**20-POUND DOG**	**40-POUND DOG**	**60-POUND DOG**	**80-POUND DOG**
¼ cup	⅓ cup	½ cup	⅔ cup	1 cup

Your best friend digs gardening.

PUPPY PESTO

Do you ever buy a bunch of parsley for a recipe that requires only a couple of tablespoons and then put the remaining parsley back in the fridge? A week later it's a wilted mess. Instead of letting your extra parsley go to waste, put it to use in freshening your dog's breath by sprinkling this over her dry food. The Brazil nut is a good source of selenium, and the cheese makes the combination irresistible.

1 cup chopped fresh parsley

¼ cup freshly grated Parmesan cheese

1 Brazil nut

Combine all of the ingredients in a food processor and pulse for about 20 seconds, or until the mixture is chopped to a fine texture.

Store in the refrigerator for up to 2 weeks or freeze in portions in an ice cube tray. Once frozen, the ice cubes can be stored in a plastic bag in the freezer for up to 3 months.

YIELD: about 1 cup

ALLOWANCE PER DAY				
10-POUND DOG	**20-POUND DOG**	**40-POUND DOG**	**60-POUND DOG**	**80-POUND DOG**
1 teaspoon	1 tablespoon	2 tablespoons	3 tablespoons	¼ cup

GIBLET GRAVY

Some people like to use turkey giblets in their Thanksgiving gravy, but many people just throw these nutritious morsels out. Give your dog something to be thankful for with this delicious and easy way to dress up kibble. As long as the potatoes are free of eyes or green spots, keep the skins on. The bulk of iron and calcium in potatoes is in the skin, as well as nearly one-quarter of the total nutrition.

2 medium russet potatoes

Giblets from 1 turkey, including the neck, liver, heart, and gizzard

4 cups water

¼ cup chopped fresh parsley (optional)

Cut the potatoes into quarters.

Combine the potatoes, giblets, water, and parsley, if using, in a medium pot. Bring to a boil, uncovered, and then decrease the heat to low. Simmer with the lid slightly askew for 20 minutes, or until the potatoes are tender.

Remove from the heat and strain the stock. Discard the neck. Allow the stock to cool to room temperature.

Pulse the stock, the remaining giblets, potatoes, and parsley in a blender until smooth.

Store in the refrigerator for up to 1 week or in the freezer for up to 2 months.

YIELD: 6 cups

ALLOWANCE PER DAY				
10-POUND DOG	**20-POUND DOG**	**40-POUND DOG**	**60-POUND DOG**	**80-POUND DOG**
2 tablespoons	¼ cup	⅓ cup	½ cup	⅔ cup

PUMPKIN PUREE

Small sugar pumpkins and squatty Cinderella pumpkins can be found in stores, or you can grow your own pumpkins especially for this purpose. When we cook pumpkins, I bake three or four at a time to make the process more efficient. However, once a pumpkin has been carved for Halloween, toss it in the compost pile, away from your dogs, to avoid bacteria and mold.

For your dog, pumpkin puree is the great equalizer; whether your dog is constipated or has diarrhea, the soluble fiber helps bring your dog back to center. Have a can on hand or some homemade puree in the freezer for whenever your dog's digestive tract is off track.

Preheat the oven to 350°F.

1 (3- to 4-pound) pumpkin

Wash the outside of the pumpkin and cut it into quarters. Scoop out the inside with a heavy metal spoon and discard the fibers. (Toast the seeds using the recipe that follows and share them with your dog.)

Place the pumpkin quarters flesh side down in the bottom of a large roasting pan or on a rimmed baking sheet and roast for 45 minutes, until the flesh is tender.

Allow the pumpkin to cool, and then scoop out the flesh and discard the skin.

Puree the pumpkin in batches in a food processor for about 30 seconds, until smooth, or mash with a potato masher.

If using the puree in recipes, place in a fine-mesh sieve to drain excess liquid for 5 minutes, or until the mixture has thickened. (You can pour the liquid over dry dog food.)

The pumpkin puree can be kept in the refrigerator for up to 1 week or in the freezer for up to 6 months.

YIELD: 2 to 3 cups

ALLOWANCE PER DAY				
10-POUND DOG	**20-POUND DOG**	**40-POUND DOG**	**60-POUND DOG**	**80-POUND DOG**
1 tablespoon	3 tablespoons	¼ cup	⅓ cup	½ cup

PUMPKIN SEEDS

The secret to crunchy seeds is boiling them first. If you don't feel like boiling the seeds first, spread them out on a baking sheet and let them sit overnight before baking. Your dog can snack on them after baking, or you can pulse them in a food processor first; they are a natural remedy for preventing or eliminating worms. This recipe uses a modest amount of garlic salt for flavoring, but garlic powder can also be used as a low-sodium alternative.

Preheat the oven to 275°F.

Raw pumpkin seeds from 1 pumpkin

Clean the strings and flesh from the seeds, then rinse them in cold water.

6 cups water

Add the water and pumpkin seeds to a medium pot and bring to a boil. Simmer for 10 minutes, then drain.

2 tablespoons olive oil

¼ teaspoon garlic salt

Combine the seeds, olive oil, and garlic salt on a rimmed baking sheet and toss to coat.

Bake for 45 to 50 minutes, until lightly toasted.

Store the seeds in an airtight container at room temperature for up to 1 month.

YIELD: 3 to 4 cups from a 3-pound pumpkin

ALLOWANCE PER DAY				
10-POUND DOG	**20-POUND DOG**	**40-POUND DOG**	**60-POUND DOG**	**80-POUND DOG**
½ teaspoon	1 teaspoon	1½ teaspoons	2 teaspoons	1 tablespoon

COOKIES

The word *cookie* brings every dog's ears to full attention. Whether it's the crunch of a dry biscuit that reminds your dog of an afternoon chewing on a bone or the essence of meat imbued with a homemade stock, cookies are fantastic after-dinner treats or post-walk rewards for good behavior.

Every piece of food you give your dog carries a message: Thank you, I care for you, I want to share this with you. The message often gets lost in the process as we hand over the treat and our dogs go off to make a pile of crumbs on the carpet. Your dog is focusing on the cookie, not you. Whether it's in training or just while spending time together, people often just hand over another cookie, which leads to additional weight gain, and the intended message is lost.

Try this two-minute experiment with your best friend:

- Take a couple of cookies and break them into 6 or 8 pieces.
- Have your dog sit in front of you.
- When your dog is settled and calm, give him one piece of cookie.
- After all the chewing and chop licking of that first bite is finished, wait for your dog to concentrate on you again.
- When your dog is settled and calm, hand over another piece of cookie.
- Repeat until all the cookie pieces are gone, and then show your dogs the palms of your hand as the "all gone" sign.

During this time, your dog is not just enjoying the cookie; he's also focusing on you as you slowly dole out one bite after another. If one year is like seven years to a dog, you just spent the equivalent of 14 dog minutes making your best friend's day special.

In the same vein, unless you're giving cookies as a gift and want a more attractive look, rather than spending time shaping cookies into bone shapes, use a pizza cutter to quickly cut them into 1-inch squares and spend the time you save with your best friend. Another quick way of making a prettier cookie for gifts is to use a ravioli cutter with fluted edges.

A variety of whole-grain flours are used throughout these recipes. Try incorporating them into your own baking, as they can be healthier alternatives to processed white flour. Many of these flours have a higher oil content, which decreases their shelf life, so purchase the quantities you need from bulk bins or store in the refrigerator to prevent spoilage. When substituting a different type of flour, the amount needed can vary from 75 to 125 percent, so you may have to start slowly and experiment to find what works best.

The following flours, which contain gluten, tend to be easier to work with when baking cookies:

- Whole-wheat flour is more nutritious and has a nuttier taste than refined white flour, though it tends to need more liquid to provide the same results.
- Barley flour is slightly sweeter than wheat flour, and it can be substituted for an equal amount of wheat flour.

- Rye flour creates dense, moist cookies with lots of flavor.
- Spelt flour absorbs liquids more readily than wheat flour, so use up to 25 percent less liquid.

Gluten-free flours are prized for causing fewer interactions for wheat-sensitive pets, but they often have tradeoffs:

- Amaranth flour has a high protein content and is usually best used in combination with other flours.
- Buckwheat flour, contrary to its name, does not contain wheat or gluten. It has a strong flavor and can be substituted for an equal amount of wheat flour.
- Cornmeal is not used in any of the cookie recipes in this book, but it can be included in small amounts to give an interesting texture. Cookies with larger quantities of cornmeal may have difficulty retaining their shape.
- Garbanzo (or chickpea) flour is high in digestible protein and has a lower glycemic index. Use 10 to 15 percent less garbanzo flour when substituting for whole-wheat flour.
- Millet flour is easy to digest and creates a tender cookie, but it should be purchased in small quantities, as it may spoil quickly.
- Oat flour is gluten free but should be certified on the label as such if gluten is a concern, because some cross-contamination can occur during production. Oat flour can create a gummy dough but results in a tender cookie.
- Quinoa flour is high in minerals and protein but may need to be used in conjunction with other flours for best results.
- Rice flour can create a grainy product that does not retain its shape well, so consider combining it with oat flour when using in recipes.

The cookie recipes here also include a range of baking times that will provide different results:

- Shorter baking times will provide a soft cookie. These are ideal for older dogs, those with dental problems, or dogs who just like something chewy rather than crunchy. Because of their higher moisture content, these cookies should be stored in an airtight container in the refrigerator or freezer.
- Longer baking times provide a crunchy, dry cookie. These are my favorites for stuffing into a Kong or snapping into smaller pieces to provide training rewards. Store crunchy cookies in an airtight container at room temperature for up to 2 weeks.
- Baking powder is included in many of the cookie recipes to create a puffier cookie that is easier for dogs to crunch into when the cookies are baked a little longer. However, this ingredient is optional.

Your best friend doesn't play tennis with tennis balls.

EASY CHEESIES

Rice flour is a gluten-free option that can be difficult to work with because it doesn't help dough maintain its shape very well. Using eggs and cheese helps this dough hold together, and rolling it out directly onto a baking sheet makes it easy to prepare.

2 cups rice flour, plus more for rolling out

1½ cups loosely packed grated cheddar cheese

1 tablespoon dried oregano

2 large eggs

½ cup Beef, Chicken, or Fish Stock (pages 65–67)

3 tablespoons canola oil

Preheat the oven to 300°F. Dust a baking sheet lightly with rice flour.

In a large bowl, toss the rice flour, cheese, and oregano together by hand until blended.

Add the eggs, stock, and oil to the flour mixture and blend with a fork. Once the mixture is blended, knead briefly to gather into a ball and transfer directly to the baking sheet. Flatten the ball and shape into a square.

Dust the top of the dough with additional rice flour and roll into a 10-inch square. Then cut with a pizza cutter into 1-inch squares.

Bake for 35 minutes for a soft cookie or up to 50 minutes for a drier cookie.

Remove from the oven and allow the cookies to cool on the baking sheet before breaking them apart at the cut lines.

YIELD: 100 cookies

ALLOWANCE PER DAY				
10-POUND DOG	**20-POUND DOG**	**40-POUND DOG**	**60-POUND DOG**	**80-POUND DOG**
1 cookie	2 cookies	3 cookies	4 cookies	5 cookies

GOLDEN KOI

These golden cookies don't just have the flavor of fish—they are fish. This recipe was developed for dogs fighting cancer, combining ingredients higher in protein and lower in carbohydrates than regular wheat-based cookies. The turmeric and fish will aid dogs fighting the big C. The garbanzo flour also creates a cookie that is safe for dogs with gluten allergies. The drier this cookie is, the less you'll smell it when you open the cookie jar.

DON'T SPLATTER!

When opening a sardine can, don't take the lid completely off; leaving a small connection between container and lid intact will prevent it from snapping off and splattering all over you.

Preheat the oven to 325°F. Lightly dust a baking sheet with garbanzo flour.

1 (3.5-ounce) can sardines, packed in tomato sauce

1 large egg

¼ cup water

1 teaspoon ground turmeric

Using a fork, blend the sardines, egg, water, and turmeric in a medium bowl until the sardines are reduced to a fine texture.

2½ cups garbanzo flour, plus more for rolling out

¼ cup canola oil

Stir the garbanzo flour and oil into the sardine mixture with a wooden spoon until the mixture comes together.

Knead briefly to gather the dough into a ball and transfer directly to the baking sheet. Flatten the ball and shape into a square.

Dust the top of the dough with additional garbanzo flour and roll into a 10-inch square. Then cut with a pizza cutter into 1-inch squares.

Bake for 30 to 35 minutes, until lightly browned and dry.

Remove from the oven and allow the cookies to cool on the baking sheet before breaking them apart at the cut lines.

YIELD: 100 cookies

ALLOWANCE PER DAY				
10-POUND DOG	**20-POUND DOG**	**40-POUND DOG**	**60-POUND DOG**	**80-POUND DOG**
2 cookies	4 cookies	6 cookies	8 cookies	10 cookies

PEANUT BUTTER AND CINNAMON COOKIES

Some dogs love the taste of peanut butter. Here, it's combined with cinnamon, which contains antioxidants and anti-inflammatory properties. The scent of the cinnamon and peanut butter baking is heavenly, and will certainly bring curious noses sniffing around. If your local grocery store has freshly ground peanut butter available, try it in these treats to make them healthier; it has fewer additives and is sugar free.

MAKE YOUR OWN PEANUT BUTTER

Make your own peanut butter by combining ½ cup unsalted dry-roasted peanuts in a food processor and processing for 3 to 4 minutes, until smooth. Please note that different types of peanut butter—smooth, crunchy, natural, or homemade—may require a little more or a little less flour to achieve the same results in a recipe.

Preheat the oven to 300°F. Lightly dust a baking sheet with flour.

½ cup unsalted peanut butter

¾ cup Beef, Chicken, or Fish Stock (pages 65–67)

In a medium bowl, melt the peanut butter and stock for 40 seconds on high power in the microwave. Stir until the peanut butter is melted evenly into the stock.

2 cups whole-wheat flour, plus more for rolling out

1 teaspoon baking powder

1 teaspoon ground cinnamon

Add the flour, baking powder, and cinnamon to the peanut butter mixture and stir with a spatula until the dough begins to gather together. Form into a ball and knead briefly until smooth.

Transfer directly to the baking sheet. Flatten the ball and shape into a square.

Dust the top of the dough with additional flour and roll into a 10-inch square. Then cut with a pizza cutter into 1-inch squares.

Bake for 20 minutes for a soft cookie or up to 35 minutes for a crisper cookie.

Remove from the oven and allow the cookies to cool on the baking sheet before breaking them apart at the cut lines.

YIELD: 100 cookies

ALLOWANCE PER DAY				
10-POUND DOG	**20-POUND DOG**	**40-POUND DOG**	**60-POUND DOG**	**80-POUND DOG**
2 cookies	4 cookies	6 cookies	8 cookies	10 cookies

Your best friend runs a six-legged race.

LIVERIFFIC COOKIES

This recipe uses chicken liver, which has a lighter scent than beef liver, making it nicer for you and still heavenly for your dog. This is a great cookie for stuffing in a Kong, because your dog will not give up until every morsel has been retrieved.

2¼ cups rye flour, plus more for rolling out

Preheat the oven to 325°F. Lightly dust a baking sheet with rye flour.

1 teaspoon baking powder

½ cup water

½ cup chicken livers

3 tablespoons canola oil

Combine all of the ingredients in a food processor and pulse for about 1 minute, or until the dough comes together in a ball.

Knead briefly to gather the dough into a ball and transfer directly to the baking sheet. Flatten the ball and shape into a square.

Dust the top of the dough with additional flour and roll into a 10-inch square. Then cut with a pizza cutter into 1-inch squares.

Bake for 30 minutes for a softer cookie or up to 40 minutes for a crisper cookie.

Remove from the oven and allow the cookies to cool on the baking sheet before breaking them apart at the cut lines.

YIELD: 100 cookies

ALLOWANCE PER DAY				
10-POUND DOG	**20-POUND DOG**	**40-POUND DOG**	**60-POUND DOG**	**80-POUND DOG**
2 cookies	4 cookies	6 cookies	8 cookies	10 cookies

PUP'S PARMESAN COOKIES

Why let the leftover chunk of Parmesan you used for pasta just sit in the back of the fridge and get moldy? If you have an extra nub, you can easily transform it into grated cheese using a Microplane grater. You'll barely notice a square inch of cheese missing from the block, and your dog will love these delicious cookies.

Preheat the oven to 325°F. Lightly dust a baking sheet with flour.

2 cups whole-wheat flour, plus more for rolling out

Whisk the flour, baking powder, and rosemary in a large bowl.

1 tablespoon baking powder

1 tablespoon finely chopped fresh rosemary

¾ cup Beef, Chicken, or Fish Stock (pages 65–67)

Add the stock, oil, and cheese to the dry ingredients and stir with a spoon until the dough starts to gather together. Form into a ball and knead briefly until smooth.

3 tablespoons canola oil

¼ cup freshly grated Parmesan cheese

Transfer directly to the baking sheet. Flatten the ball and shape into a square.

Dust the top of the dough with additional flour and roll into a 10-inch square. Then cut with a pizza cutter into 1-inch squares.

Bake for 25 minutes for a softer cookie or up to 40 minutes for a crisper cookie.

Remove from the oven and allow the cookies to cool on the baking sheet before breaking them apart at the cut lines.

YIELD: 100 cookies

ALLOWANCE PER DAY				
10-POUND DOG	**20-POUND DOG**	**40-POUND DOG**	**60-POUND DOG**	**80-POUND DOG**
2 cookies	4 cookies	6 cookies	8 cookies	10 cookies

GREEN PEA CHRISTMAS TREES

When it comes to the annual Christmas cookie exchange, consider bringing cookies for those that Santa sometimes forgets: the dogs of your friends and coworkers. Combining two easy-to-digest ingredients like peas and fennel makes this cookie a tummy pleaser. Other flours, like buckwheat or gluten-free oat flour, can be substituted for the wheat flour to make a heartier or gluten-free cookie. Adding ½ cup of dried cranberries to the food processor with the dry ingredients and using spinach juice in place of the stock will provide even more holiday cheer.

Preheat the oven to 350°F. Lightly dust a baking sheet with flour.

1 cup frozen peas

¼ cup Beef, Chicken, or Fish Stock (pages 65–67)

Combine the frozen peas and stock in a microwave-safe bowl. Microwave on high power for 2 minutes.

3 tablespoons canola oil

1 tablespoon fennel seeds

Add the pea mixture, canola oil, and fennel seeds to a food processor and pulse until the mixture is smooth, about 1 minute.

2 cups whole-wheat flour, plus more for rolling out

1 tablespoon baking powder

Add the flour and baking powder and pulse for about 1 minute, or until the dough gathers into a ball.

Gather the dough into a ball and transfer directly to the baking sheet. Flatten the ball and shape into a square.

Dust the top of the dough with additional flour and roll into a 10-inch square. Then cut with a pizza cutter into 1-inch squares, or cut out Christmas trees with a cookie cutter and transfer to a flour-dusted baking sheet, about ½ inch apart.

Bake for 30 minutes for a softer cookie or up to 45 minutes for a drier cookie.

Remove from the oven and allow the cookies to cool on the baking sheet. Break apart at the cut lines if you have made squares.

YIELD: 100 cookies

ALLOWANCE PER DAY				
10-POUND DOG	**20-POUND DOG**	**40-POUND DOG**	**60-POUND DOG**	**80-POUND DOG**
2 cookies	4 cookies	6 cookies	8 cookies	10 cookies

Your best friend is a licensed copilot.

TOOT SWEETS

Yucca schidigera *powder is an extract of the Mojave yucca that is an increasingly common ingredient in animal feed and pet treats. It is a strong anti-inflammatory, helps many dogs produce less gas, and can keep your grass a little greener by reducing the ammonia in feces and urine naturally. Oat flour is also easy for dogs to digest, and will help prevent gas.*

½ cup Beef, Chicken, or Fish Stock (pages 65–67)

1 cup chopped fresh parsley

2 tablespoons canola oil

2 cups oat flour, plus more for rolling out

1¼ teaspoons *Yucca schidigera* powder

¼ cup nutritional yeast

🐾 Preheat the oven to 300°F. Lightly dust a baking sheet with flour.

🐾 Combine all of the ingredients in a large bowl and stir until the dough gathers together.

Knead briefly to gather the dough into a ball and transfer directly to the baking sheet. Flatten the ball and shape into a square.

Dust the top of the dough with additional flour and roll into a 10-inch square. Then cut with a pizza cutter into 1-inch squares.

Bake for 45 minutes, or until lightly browned, to create a firm cookie, as baking for less time may result in crumbly cookies.

Remove from the oven and allow the cookies to cool on the baking sheet before breaking them apart at the cut lines.

🐾 **YIELD:** 100 cookies

I've found the recommended amount listed by some manufacturers to be a bit excessive. If you'd like to add Yucca schidigera *powder to your dog's diet on its own, look for capsules that provide the following amounts: For dogs 1 to 15 pounds: 25 milligrams*

For dogs 16 to 30 pounds: 50 milligrams

For dogs 31 to 70 pounds: 75 milligrams

For dogs over 70 pounds: 100 milligrams

Yucca schidigera *powder can be found at pet stores, health-food stores, or from the online resources listed on page 190.*

ALLOWANCE PER DAY				
10-POUND DOG	20-POUND DOG	40-POUND DOG	60-POUND DOG	80-POUND DOG
2 cookies	4 cookies	6 cookies	8 cookies	10 cookies

BARKSCOTTI

These cookies pack a lot of flavor into their little domed shapes and when sliced thin are great for breaking into bits or stuffing into a Kong for a long-lasting treat. Like biscotti, this recipe creates a hard, crunchy cookie.

Preheat the oven to 300°F.

⅔ cup Beef Stock (page 65)

Heat the Beef Stock for about 2 minutes, or until warm to hot, in the microwave.

½ cup grated carrots
½ cup finely chopped fresh parsley
½ teaspoon garlic powder

Combine the carrots, parsley, and garlic powder in a large bowl. Pour the hot stock over the vegetables and allow to sit for a few minutes, until soft.

1 cup barley flour
3 tablespoons olive oil
1 tablespoon baking powder
1 cup rye flour

Stir the barley flour, olive oil, and baking powder into the vegetable mixture until blended. Mix in the rye flour until fully incorporated.

Turn out the dough onto a lightly floured board. Knead the dough for about 2 minutes, or until smooth.

Shape the dough into a loaf that's 16 inches long by 3 inches wide and about ½ inch in height, smoothing the edges to form the loaf into a dome shape.

Cut dough widthwise into strips about ⅓ inch thick.

Stand individual cookies on a baking sheet, domed side up, about 1 inch apart.

Bake for 1 hour, then turn the oven off and let the cookies rest in the oven for 1 hour longer. Remove from the oven and let cool on the baking sheet.

YIELD: 48 cookies

ALLOWANCE PER DAY				
10-POUND DOG	**20-POUND DOG**	**40-POUND DOG**	**60-POUND DOG**	**80-POUND DOG**
1 cookie	2 cookies	3 cookies	4 cookies	5 cookies

FRESH KISS COOKIES

Dogs love us, so they're going to try and kiss us, no matter how much we protest. These cookies not only make those kisses more tolerable, they'll also increase your dog's desire to say thank you. Get those kisses early, before your dog starts to drool.

🐾 Preheat the oven to 300°F. Lightly flour a baking sheet.

1 cup Beef, Chicken, or Fish Stock (pages 65–67)

🐾 Heat the stock for about 2 minutes, or until boiling, in the microwave.

1 cup finely chopped fresh parsley

🐾 Combine the parsley, mint, canola oil, and stock in a large bowl.

1 cup finely chopped fresh mint

2 tablespoons canola oil

2⅓ cups whole-wheat flour, plus more for rolling out

🐾 Stir the flour into the herb mixture until blended.

Turn out the dough onto a lightly floured board. Knead the dough for about 2 minutes, or until smooth.

Knead briefly to gather the dough into a ball and transfer directly to the baking sheet. Flatten the ball and shape into a square.

Dust the top of the dough with additional flour and roll into a 10-inch square. Then cut with a pizza cutter into 1-inch squares.

Bake for 25 minutes for a soft cookie or up to 45 minutes for a crunchy cookie.

Remove from the oven and allow the cookies to cool on the baking sheet before breaking them apart at the cut lines.

🐾 **YIELD:** 100 cookies

ALLOWANCE PER DAY				
10-POUND DOG	**20-POUND DOG**	**40-POUND DOG**	**60-POUND DOG**	**80-POUND DOG**
2 cookies	4 cookies	6 cookies	8 cookies	10 cookies

GINGERBREAD MAILMAN COOKIES

There your dog was, taking a nap, when all of a sudden the mail carrier comes by to drop off the mail. It only makes sense that a dog would bark like crazy to defend his territory, even if it's all for naught. Here's a little sweet revenge in the form of a gingerbread cookie. Remember to judge your serving size appropriately if you're shaping these into gingerbread men; for small dogs, a typical serving might just be an arm or a leg depending on the size of your cookie cutter.

Preheat the oven to 325°F.

1 cup whole-wheat flour
1 cup all-purpose flour
1 teaspoon baking powder
1 teaspoon ground cinnamon
½ teaspoon ground ginger

Combine the flours, baking powder, cinnamon, and ginger in a large bowl.

⅓ cup Chicken Stock (page 66) or water
⅓ cup blackstrap molasses
3 tablespoons canola oil
Nonstick cooking spray

Add the stock, molasses, and oil to the dry ingredients and stir until fully mixed. (Wipe the inside of the measuring cup for the molasses with a little of the oil first to prevent the molasses from sticking.)

Knead briefly to gather the dough into a ball.

Spray a baking sheet with nonstick cooking spray.

Roll the dough out on a lightly floured surface into a 10-inch square. If making shaped cookies, cut out with a cookie cutter and place onto the baking sheet, separated by ½ inch. If making squares, transfer the dough to the baking sheet and cut into 1-inch squares with a pizza cutter.

Bake for 25 minutes, or until crisp and dry. Allow the cookies to cool on the baking sheet and then break them apart at the cut lines if necessary.

YIELD: 100 cookies

ALLOWANCE PER DAY (1-INCH SQUARE COOKIES)				
10-POUND DOG	**20-POUND DOG**	**40-POUND DOG**	**60-POUND DOG**	**80-POUND DOG**
2 cookies	4 cookies	6 cookies	8 cookies	10 cookies

BLUEBERRY MOONS

If you've already shared some blueberry pancakes with your dog (page 42), you've seen how much she enjoyed that treat. Here's a crisp little cookie that will make your dog jump over the moon in anticipation. With all the antioxidants in the blueberries and cinnamon, you might find your dog jumping just a bit higher!

🐾 Preheat the oven to 325°F.

1 cup frozen blueberries

¼ cup Beef, Chicken, or Fish Stock (pages 65–67)

🐾 Microwave the blueberries and water in a microwave-safe bowl on high power for 2 minutes.

3 tablespoons canola oil

2 cups whole-wheat flour

1 teaspoon baking powder

1 teaspoon ground cinnamon

🐾 Combine the blueberry mixture, canola oil, flour, baking powder, and cinnamon in a food processor and pulse for about 1 minute, or until the mixture gathers into a ball.

Roll the dough out on a lightly floured surface into a 10-inch square. Transfer to a baking sheet and cut into 1-inch squares with a pizza cutter.

Bake for 25 minutes for a soft cookie or up to 40 minutes for a crunchy cookie.

Remove from the oven and allow the cookies to cool on the baking sheet before breaking them apart at the cut lines.

🐾 **YIELD:** 100 cookies

ALLOWANCE PER DAY (1-INCH SQUARE COOKIES)				
10-POUND DOG	**20-POUND DOG**	**40-POUND DOG**	**60-POUND DOG**	**80-POUND DOG**
2 cookies	4 cookies	6 cookies	8 cookies	10 cookies

Your best friend tugs without war.

SOFT OATMEAL COOKIES

Here's a nice soft cookie for senior dogs with more sensitive mouths or dogs who have just returned home after a dental cleaning. With two sources of apples and sweetness from blackstrap molasses, these cookies are full of flavor and vitamins, plus they have a healthy dose of fiber to keep your pup full between meals.

Nonstick cooking spray 🐾 Preheat the oven to 350°F. Spray a baking sheet with cooking spray.

1 large egg 🐾 Combine the egg, applesauce, canola oil, and molasses in a large bowl and stir to blend.

½ cup unsweetened applesauce

2 tablespoons canola oil

2 tablespoons blackstrap molasses

1 cup whole-wheat flour 🐾 Add the flour, oats, baking powder, and apple to the egg mixture and stir with a spoon until well blended.

1 cup quick-cooking rolled oats

1 teaspoon baking powder

1 red apple (Braeburn or red Rome), cored and finely chopped

Using two spoons, scoop up 1 tablespoon of cookie dough and use the second spoon to scrape the dough onto the prepared baking sheet. Place the cookies 1 inch apart.

Bake for 15 minutes, or until lightly browned. Transfer the cookies to a wire rack and allow them to cool for 20 minutes.

Because these are soft cookies, store in the refrigerator for up to 1 week or in the freezer for up to 2 months.

🐾 **YIELD:** 48 cookies

ALLOWANCE PER DAY				
10-POUND DOG	**20-POUND DOG**	**40-POUND DOG**	**60-POUND DOG**	**80-POUND DOG**
1 cookie	2 cookies	3 cookies	4 cookies	5 cookies

BACON YAPPETIZERS

It seems the best appetizers at a party are always wrapped in bacon. Using a small amount of bacon grease and cooked crumbled bacon imbues this treat with a scent that drives canine party guests crazy. If you want to get fancy about it, you can top them with a little grated Parmesan cheese while they are warm. Nutritional yeast is added for a good dose of B vitamins and combined with the garlic powder to ward off the worst kind of party guest—fleas.

Preheat the oven to 350°F. Lightly dust a baking sheet with flour.

2 slices bacon

Cook the bacon in the microwave for 3 minutes on high power or in a skillet over medium heat until crisp. Drain the bacon and reserve 2 tablespoons of bacon grease.

2 cups rye flour, plus more for rolling out

¼ cup nutritional yeast

1 tablespoon baking powder

½ teaspoon garlic powder

Mix the flour, yeast, baking powder, and garlic powder together in a large bowl.

⅔ cup Beef Stock (page 65)

Mix the stock and reserved bacon grease together, and then mix into the dry ingredients.

Crumble the bacon and blend into the mixture.

Knead briefly to gather the dough into a ball and transfer directly to the baking sheet. Flatten the ball and shape into a square.

Dust the top of the dough with additional flour and roll into a 10-inch square. Then cut with a pizza cutter into 1-inch squares.

Bake for 20 minutes, or until firm. Allow the cookies to cool on the baking sheet, then break them apart at the cut lines.

YIELD: 100 cookies

ALLOWANCE PER DAY				
10-POUND DOG	**20-POUND DOG**	**40-POUND DOG**	**60-POUND DOG**	**80-POUND DOG**
1 cookie	2 cookies	4 cookies	6 cookies	8 cookies

MEALS

MOTHER HUBBARD EGGS
AND OATMEAL

ARROZ CON POLLO

CHICKEN FOR PUPLINGS

CLUCK AND QUINOA CASSEROLE

POULTRY PALOOZA

CHICKEN THIGHS AND TABBOULEH

SLOW-COOKED CHICKEN
AND BARLEY

STIR-FRY AND RICE

TURKEY MINESTRONE

LAZYSAGNE

TURKEY MEAT LOAF

T.O.P. OF THE MORNING (TURKEY
AND OAT PORRIDGE)

BEEF AND BULGUR

BIRTHDAY BEEFCAKE
(OR PUPCAKES)

HEARTY BEEF

BEEF AND MAC (WITH JUST
A BIT OF CHEESE)

MUTT LOAF

BEEF AND POTATOES

HAMBURGER (AND MORE) PATTIES

TINY TUNA NOODLE CASSEROLE

LAMB MUFFINS

SCOTCH BROTH

PORK AND PENNE

RABBIT STEW

KIBBLE WORTH CHEWING

We have four dogs at home, so to make things easier for us we feed our dogs homemade meals in conjunction with high-quality commercial foods. The commercial food also helps us regulate cost and how much time we spend in the kitchen rather than out walking our dogs. We supplement their diet with fresh vegetables, homemade treats, and even a tiny bit of cheese every now and then. Necessary vitamins and minerals are met with their kibble, while the homemade food provides variety, freshness, and hundreds of nutrients forgotten in commercial food.

In addition to supplementation, providing a variety of foods will help to supply natural sources of the necessary nutrients. The largest difference between food for humans and food for our pets is that we allow ourselves diversity, yet insist that our pets maintain one diet for life. Ask a veterinarian, a breeder, or your specialty pet store and almost everyone will not only point you in the direction of one type of food, they'll also tell you not to switch foods for fear of causing digestive issues or diarrhea. When this is said, it's really in reference to commercial foods. Like many people, I've occasionally switched from one commercial food to another too quickly and had to deal with the resulting diarrhea. There is not much research on what exactly causes digestive upset when switching between commercial foods, but with the average dry food containing around 50 different ingredients, any one of them could be the culprit. Commercial food should always be transitioned slowly.

If you're just starting your dog out on fresh food, it's best to take a cautious approach as well. As you see how well your dog tolerates different fresh foods, try transitioning in other meals. A wide variety of meals are included throughout this book so that you can find choices that you enjoy making and your pet enjoys eating.

I have a great deal of respect for raw diets because they can be a good alternative for many pets. However, I have not included recipes for raw diets because I feel that these are best prepared commercially. Modern meat production has some safeguards, yet we still hear about recalls because of unsafe levels of bacteria. Meat purchased at the grocery store is not graded or monitored for raw consumption. There are a lot of bacteria in fresh meat that are killed when meats are cooked to the proper temperature but can cause illness in both humans and dogs when consumed raw. Raw-food manufacturers must continually test their ingredients to ensure bacteria levels are safe, whereas the same tests are not done at the butcher's counter.

Many people are concerned about the heavy use of grain in commercial dog foods, and I'm right there with them. Foods that rely on grains to provide the bulk of your dog's nutrition and then include only a slight amount of meat products are not my favorite choices. At the other end of the spectrum, we must also consider that meat-based diets take a heavy toll on our environment, and it seems a little backward to feed your dog more meat than you are eating yourself. Grains can be good providers of energy, fiber, and nutrients when used in moderation. They help to slow down digestion, make your dog feel a little fuller, and are lower in calories than meats. However, I avoid feeding my dogs commercial foods made with corn products because those products tend to be more corn than anything else.

TIPS FOR COOKING FOR YOUR BEST FRIEND

- Grind or shred vegetables and fruit with a food processor. It's easier for your dog to digest, the vegetables cook faster, and the smaller a vegetable is, the less likely that your dog will pick it out.
- Cook grains with the meat or in homemade stock so that they absorb more of the flavor. Rice on its own is pretty bland and not so interesting to your dog, but chicken-flavored rice tastes like rice made from chicken.
- Meals that are designed for regular feeding have been adjusted to be 3,600 calories overall, so they will always provide the same amount of servings. Serving sizes are broken out for active dogs at 10, 20, 40, 60, and 80 pounds. If your dog's caloric needs are different, divide the calories your dog needs per day by the calories per cup noted in each recipe to determine how many cups per day your dog should be fed.
- All recipes can be halved, doubled, quadrupled, or adjusted to whatever size your pots can hold. Cooking in bulk saves you time and money. Just be sure to adjust the cooking times to ensure that all ingredients are thoroughly cooked. If you are adjusting a recipe, go ahead and write the adjusted amounts in the margin to ensure that all ingredients remain in the correct proportions.
- If you're supplementing with a vitamin and your dog won't eat the vitamin by itself, grind up the tablet in a clean coffee grinder. To clean the coffee grinder out really well, process some dry white rice in the grinder for a few seconds and then brush it out with a pastry brush.
- Meals can be refrigerated for up to 4 days. Freeze any additional portions in containers that fit 2 to 3 days' worth of food for convenience, and divvy up accordingly at mealtime.
- Great deals on meat can be found at warehouse stores, restaurant suppliers, and Asian specialty markets (for special cuts of meat).
- If you value sustainable and organic ingredients for yourself, it makes sense to extend the benefits to your own dog. You can honor the animals that provide nutrition to both you and your dog by purchasing humanely raised meat.

Your best friend is stirred by home cooking.

MOTHER HUBBARD EGGS AND OATMEAL

It happens to everyone sometime: You look at your spouse and say, "Didn't you go to the store?" If you're out of dog food and the store is closed or you're rushing off to work, you can still provide a quick warm meal for your dog. This is an incredibly simple meal that requires just two trips to the microwave until you can make a trip to the store.

	10-POUND DOG	20-POUND DOG	40-POUND DOG	60-POUND DOG	80-POUND DOG
Egg	1 large	1 large	2 large	3 large	3 large
Water	2 tablespoons	⅓ cup	½ cup	½ cup	⅔ cup
Oatmeal	¼ cup	½ cup	¾ cup	1 cup	1 cup
Carrots, apples, or green beans	¼ cup	½ cup	¾ cup	¾ cup	1 cup
COOKING TIME	2 minutes	2½ minutes	3 minutes	3½ minutes	4½ minutes
SERVINGS	1 meal	1 meal	1 meal	1 meal	1 meal

🐾 Spray a microwave-safe bowl with cooking spray.

🐾 Mix the egg and water in a medium bowl until blended.

🐾 Blend in the oatmeal, and then layer the vegetables over the top so that they will steam and the oatmeal will be able to absorb the liquid.

🐾 Cook for the appropriate amount of time according to the chart.

🐾 Fluff the mixture and allow the dish to cool for 5 to 10 minutes prior to serving.

ARROZ CON POLLO

A popular dish in Latin American countries, arroz con pollo (rice with chicken) will also be a popular choice in your dog's bowl. Typically this dish is made with a sofrito, a mix of peppers, garlic, and onions. We leave out the onion because of the dangers to your pet, but keep the healthy choices of red bell pepper, garlic, and tomatoes. There's lots of flavor in this dish and your dog won't need a passport to enjoy it.

¼ cup olive oil

1 pound boneless, skinless chicken thighs, diced

Heat the oil over medium-high heat in a large pot. Add the chicken and cook for 8 minutes, stirring occasionally.

1 red bell pepper, seeded and chopped

2 teaspoons dried oregano

2 teaspoons dried rosemary

¼ teaspoon garlic powder

Stir in the bell pepper, oregano, rosemary, and garlic powder and cook for 1 minute.

2 tablespoons canola oil

1 (28-ounce) can crushed tomatoes

6 cups water

3 cups long-grain white rice

Add the canola oil, tomatoes, water, and rice. Bring to a low boil over high heat, then decrease the heat to low and cook for 20 minutes, or until the rice is very tender. Stir occasionally to prevent any rice from sticking to the bottom of the pot.

Remove from the heat and allow the stew to cool prior to mixing in any supplements.

¼ cup chopped fresh parsley (optional)

Add the parsley, if desired, and stir to mix.

YIELD: 13 cups; 275 calories per cup

DAILY PORTION				
Divide into two meals, or serve one-half the daily portion per day with one-half the normal amount of dry food.				
10-POUND DOG	**20-POUND DOG**	**40-POUND DOG**	**60-POUND DOG**	**80-POUND DOG**
1 to 1¼ cups	1⅔ to 2 cups	2⅔ to 3½ cups	3⅔ to 4⅔ cups	4⅔ to 6 cups

CHICKEN FOR PUPLINGS

There's nothing like a warm bowl of chicken and dumplings to take away the winter chills. This version replaces the dumplings with chunks of potatoes, so it's perfect for dogs who need to avoid gluten.

3 tablespoons olive oil

3 pounds boneless, skinless chicken thighs, cut into ½-inch cubes

In a large stockpot, heat the oil over medium-high heat. Add the chicken and stir occasionally until all pieces are lightly browned, about 8 minutes.

1 tablespoon dried rosemary

¼ teaspoon garlic powder

Add the rosemary and garlic powder and stir until fragrant, about 1 minute.

4 cups Chicken Stock (page 66)

1 cup grated carrots

3 pounds potatoes, skin on, cleaned of eyes and green spots, diced into ½-inch cubes

1 cup frozen peas

Stir in the stock, carrots, potatoes, and peas. Decrease the heat to medium-low and cook for 20 minutes, or until the potatoes are tender.

Remove from the heat and allow the stew to cool prior to mixing in any supplements.

YIELD: 14 cups; 260 calories per cup

DAILY PORTION

Divide into two meals, or serve one-half the daily portion per day with one-half the normal amount of dry food.

10-POUND DOG	20-POUND DOG	40-POUND DOG	60-POUND DOG	80-POUND DOG
1 to 1⅓ cups	1⅔ to 2⅓ cups	3 to 4 cups	4 to 5¼ cups	5 to 6½ cups

CLUCK AND QUINOA CASSEROLE

We often think of a meat loaf as made of beef, but it's just as easy, nutritious, and tasty for your dog when it's made from chicken. Quinoa is the seed from a relative of the spinach family and was a staple food of the Incas. Today, quinoa is being rediscovered in healthy recipes for people because it is packed with protein, iron, potassium, and B vitamins. Quinoa also contains metabolites called saponins, which are believed to have anti-cancer and anti-inflammatory benefits. Try this grain for your dog and for yourself.

Nonstick cooking spray	Preheat the oven to 350°F and spray a 9 by 13-inch baking dish with nonstick cooking spray.
3 cups Chicken Stock (page 66)	Mix all of the remaining ingredients in a large bowl until thoroughly combined.
1½ cups quinoa	Lightly spoon the mixture into the prepared baking dish.
3 pounds ground chicken	Bake for 1 hour, or until all of the liquid has been absorbed.
4 large eggs, beaten	Remove from the oven and allow the casserole to cool prior to mixing in any supplements.
1 cup grated carrots	
1 cup grated zucchini	**YIELD:** 14 cups; 280 calories per cup
1 tablespoon olive oil	

DAILY PORTION

Divide into two meals, or serve one-half the daily portion per day with one-half the normal amount of dry food.

10-POUND DOG	20-POUND DOG	40-POUND DOG	60-POUND DOG	80-POUND DOG
1 to 1¼ cups	1⅔ to 2¼ cups	2⅔ to 3⅔ cups	4 to 5¼ cups	5 to 6½ cups

POULTRY PALOOZA

Using inexpensive cuts of chicken allows you to dish up a lot of flavor to liven up a bowl of kibble. Because this is so high in protein and phosphorus, don't forget to add the Eggshell Powder to provide enough calcium. This is best served in combination with a commercial food so that your dog receives enough of all the necessary nutrients.

3 tablespoons canola oil

Heat the oil in a large stockpot over medium heat.

3½ pounds boneless, skinless chicken thighs, diced into bite-size bits

Add the chicken thighs, gizzards, hearts, livers, rosemary, garlic powder, and water and simmer for 20 to 25 minutes, until all the meat is browned and cooked through.

1 pound chicken gizzards, chopped

1 pound chicken hearts, chopped

½ cup chopped chicken livers, about 3 ounces

1 tablespoon finely chopped fresh rosemary

¼ teaspoon garlic powder

1 cup water

2½ teaspoons Eggshell Powder (page 15)

Remove from the heat and allow the stew to cool prior to stirring in the Eggshell Powder.

YIELD: 12 cups; 300 calories per cup

DAILY PORTION

Divide into two meals, or serve one-half the daily portion per day with one-half the normal amount of dry food.

10-POUND DOG	20-POUND DOG	40-POUND DOG	60-POUND DOG	80-POUND DOG
⅔ to 1¼ cups	1½ to 2 cups	2⅔ to 3⅓ cups	3½ to 4½ cups	4½ to 5⅔ cups

CHICKEN THIGHS AND TABBOULEH

Tabbouleh is a great summer salad made with bulgur wheat, tomatoes, and mint. Preparing the bulgur wheat is simple, and this whole meal can be prepared in a little more than an hour.

6 cups Chicken Stock (page 66)	Bring the stock to a boil in a large stockpot.
3 cups bulgur wheat	Measure the bulgur wheat into a large bowl and add the boiling stock. Cover and let sit for 1 hour. The bulgur will absorb all the stock and be light and fluffy.
¼ cup canola or olive oil	Meanwhile, heat the oil over medium-high heat in the same stockpot used for the stock.
2 pounds boneless, skinless chicken thighs, cut into 1-inch dice 1 medium red bell pepper, seeded and cut into 1-inch dice	Add the chicken and bell pepper to the stockpot and stir frequently for 8 minutes, or until the chicken is cooked through and the bell pepper has softened.
2 Roma tomatoes, cut into 1-inch dice ½ cup chopped fresh parsley or mint	Remove the pot from the heat and add the tomatoes and parsley. Cover and allow the tomatoes to steam and soften until the bulgur is ready. Add the chicken mixture to the bulgur, then toss lightly to mix thoroughly. Allow to cool prior to mixing in any supplements.
	YIELD: 14 cups; 260 calories per cup

DAILY PORTION

Divide into two meals, or serve one-half the daily portion per day with one-half the normal amount of dry food.

10-POUND DOG	20-POUND DOG	40-POUND DOG	60-POUND DOG	80-POUND DOG
1 to 1⅓ cups	1⅔ to 2⅓ cups	3 to 3¾ cups	4 to 5¼ cups	5 to 6½ cups

Your best friend appreciates toasty toes.

Slow-Cooked Chicken and Barley

Dogs will love how the chicken flavor has an opportunity to blend into all the other ingredients while everything simmers together in a slow cooker. After ten minutes of prep, you can just set the slow cooker on low as you go off to work. Just make sure that curious noses can't reach the pot while you're away. Cooking the barley for a long time makes it plump and soft, which allows for an ample serving size. This is a low-fat, high-fiber meal, great for dogs on a diet.

2 ½ cups pearl barley

2 pounds boneless, skinless chicken thighs, diced

2 cups finely chopped green beans

2 large carrots, diced or shredded

2 Roma tomatoes, chopped

5 cups water

2 tablespoons canola oil

¼ teaspoon garlic powder

Combine all of the ingredients in the pot of a 6-quart slow cooker and stir well to combine and evenly distribute the ingredients.

Set the temperature to low and cook for 8 hours.

Turn off the cooker and allow the stew to cool prior to mixing in any supplements.

YIELD: 14 cups; 260 calories per cup

DAILY PORTION

Divide into two meals, or serve one-half the daily portion per day with one-half the normal amount of dry food.

10-POUND DOG	20-POUND DOG	40-POUND DOG	60-POUND DOG	80-POUND DOG
1 to 1⅓ cups	1⅔ to 2⅓ cups	3 to 3¾ cups	4 to 5¼ cups	5 to 6⅓ cups

STIR-FRY AND RICE

Cooking fresh ginger transforms some of its antioxidants (named, appropriately enough, gingerols) into two other powerful antioxidants that are not present in the raw form: shogaols and zingerones. The antioxidants provided by ginger are helpful for dogs with nausea, diarrhea, or excessive gas, and are being studied for their abilities to prevent cancer. This recipe is not only healthy, it's also incredibly easy to prepare and can share many of the same ingredients you'd use in your own stir-fry.

¼ cup canola oil
🐾 Heat the oil in a large heavy skillet over medium heat.

1¼ pounds boneless, skinless chicken thighs, cut into ½-inch dice
🐾 Add the chicken and carrots and stir-fry until the chicken is browned, about 5 minutes.

2 medium carrots, grated

6 cups cooked long-grain white rice (see Note)
🐾 Add the rice, spinach, ginger, and garlic powder and cook for 5 minutes while lightly tossing to prevent any ingredients from burning.

½ cup thawed frozen spinach

½ teaspoon grated fresh ginger

¼ teaspoon garlic powder

4 large eggs, beaten
🐾 Mix in the eggs and cook, stirring, until the eggs have set, about 2 minutes.

Remove from the heat and allow the stir-fry to cool prior to mixing in any supplements.

🐾 **YIELD:** 9 cups; 400 calories per cup

NOTE: To cook rice, combine 2 cups of rice with 4 cups of water in a medium saucepan. Bring to a boil over high heat, then decrease the heat to low and simmer for 25 minutes, or until all the water is absorbed.

DAILY PORTION

Divide into two meals, or serve one-half the daily portion per day with one-half the normal amount of dry food.

10-POUND DOG	20-POUND DOG	40-POUND DOG	60-POUND DOG	80-POUND DOG
⅔ to 1 cup	1¼ to 1½ cups	2 to 2½ cups	2⅔ to 3⅓ cups	3⅓ to 4¼ cups

TURKEY MINESTRONE

Here's a recipe for dogs who enjoy vegetables. The minute our Lhasa Apso, Baxter, hears us chopping carrots and green beans, he's hoping that minestrone is coming his way. Since this is prepared in a slow cooker, Baxter has all day to dream about his dinnertime favorite.

2 medium carrots

1 cup green beans

Chop the carrots into large chunks and combine in a food processor with the green beans. Pulse 8 to 12 times, until finely chopped. (The carrots can be grated and chopped by hand if a food processor is not available.)

¼ cup canola oil

1½ pounds ground turkey

3 large potatoes, skin on, cleaned of eyes and green spots, diced

1 cup frozen peas

1 (14.5-ounce) can cannellini beans, rinsed and drained

1 (14.5-ounce) can crushed tomatoes

2 cups dried egg noodles

¼ cup chopped fresh parsley

¼ teaspoon garlic powder

5 cups water

Combine the carrots, green beans, oil, turkey, potatoes, peas, cannellini beans, tomatoes, noodles, parsley, garlic powder, and water in the pot of a 6-quart slow cooker. Set the temperature to low and cook for 7 to 8 hours.

Turn off the cooker and allow the stew to cool prior to mixing in any supplements.

Freshly grated Parmesan cheese (optional)

Top with a bit of Parmesan, if desired, for an extra-special surprise.

YIELD: 14 cups; 260 calories per cup

DAILY PORTION

Divide into two meals, or serve one-half the daily portion per day with one-half the normal amount of dry food.

10-POUND DOG	20-POUND DOG	40-POUND DOG	60-POUND DOG	80-POUND DOG
1 to 1¼ cups plus ½ teaspoon cheese	1⅔ to 2¼ cups plus 1 teaspoon cheese	3 to 3¾ cups plus 2 teaspoons cheese	4 to 5¼ cups plus 1 tablespoon cheese	5 to 6⅓ cups plus 2 tablespoons cheese

LAZYSAGNE

Making homemade lasagne can be a pleasant way to spend a few hours on a Sunday afternoon, but dogs eat so fast that it's doubtful that the intricate layering will be appreciated. I'm more willing to make two lasagnes for Sunday night dinner. One has homemade sauce, three different cheeses, and both sweet Italian and spicy sausage. That pan goes on my dinner table. The Lazysagne version is a quick-boil, drain-and-stir version for the hounds that doesn't receive any complaints, just plenty of drooling while they wait for us to say "Mangia!"

8 cups water	Bring the water to a boil in a large stockpot.
1 pound dried egg noodles 2 pounds ground turkey	Add the noodles and turkey to the pot and allow the water to return to a boil, uncovered to prevent overflow. Decrease the heat to low and simmer for 12 minutes, stirring occasionally, until the noodles are soft (beyond al dente). Drain the noodles and turkey, reserving the broth for other pet food uses.
1 (14.5-ounce) can crushed tomatoes 1 (10-ounce) package frozen spinach, thawed 2 cups low-fat cottage cheese	Return the noodles and turkey to the pot, add all of the remaining ingredients, and stir to combine. Allow the lasagne mixture to cool to just a bit above room temperature prior to adding any supplements.
1 teaspoon dried basil 1 teaspoon dried oregano ¼ teaspoon garlic powder	**YIELD:** 16 cups; 230 calories per cup

---

DAILY PORTION

Divide into two meals, or serve one-half the daily portion per day with one-half the normal amount of dry food.

10-POUND DOG	20-POUND DOG	40-POUND DOG	60-POUND DOG	80-POUND DOG
1¼ to 1½ cups	2 to 2⅔ cups	3⅓ to 4⅓ cups	4½ to 5⅔ cups	5⅔ to 7¼ cups

TURKEY MEAT LOAF

When I first made this for the dogs I couldn't resist trying a bite, and then another. If you add a little salt and pepper, this recipe might even make it to your dinner table. The dogs like it just the way it is, and that's great because it takes less than ten minutes to mix together and then goes into the oven while I'm preparing my own dinner. With the addition of basil, garlic, and oregano, it smells pretty good too.

Preheat the oven to 350°F.

Nonstick cooking spray

Spray either two loaf pans or one 9 by 13-inch baking dish with nonstick cooking spray.

2 large eggs

1 (15-ounce) can crushed tomatoes

½ cup freshly grated Parmesan cheese

¼ cup finely chopped fresh parsley

2 teaspoons dried basil

2 teaspoons dried oregano

¼ teaspoon garlic powder

1 tablespoon soy sauce

Whisk the eggs, tomatoes, Parmesan, parsley, basil, oregano, garlic powder, and soy sauce in a large bowl until thoroughly mixed.

2½ cups quick-cooking rolled oats

2¼ pounds ground turkey

Add the oats and turkey to the egg mixture and mix thoroughly, then spoon the mixture into the prepared baking dishes.

Bake for 45 to 55 minutes, until the center of the loaf registers 170°F on a meat thermometer.

Remove from the oven and allow the meat loaf to cool prior to mixing in any supplements.

YIELD: 11 cups; 320 calories per cup

DAILY PORTION

Divide into two meals, or serve one-half the daily portion per day with one-half the normal amount of dry food.

10-POUND DOG	20-POUND DOG	40-POUND DOG	60-POUND DOG	80-POUND DOG
¾ to 1¼ cups	1½ to 2 cups	2⅓ to 3¼ cups	3⅓ to 4¼ cups	4¼ to 5¼ cups

T.O.P. OF THE MORNING (TURKEY AND OAT PORRIDGE)

Get your dog's day off to a good start with a healthy breakfast that's quick to prepare.

6 cups water

2 pounds ground turkey

¼ pound chicken liver, chopped

Bring the water to a simmer in a stockpot over medium heat and add the ground turkey and chopped chicken liver.

Simmer for 10 minutes, stirring to break up the turkey.

3 cups coarsely chopped green beans

1 tablespoon minced fresh sage

Add the green beans and sage. Simmer over low heat for an additional 5 minutes.

2¾ cups quick-cooking rolled oats

2 tablespoons safflower oil

Add the oats and oil, then remove from the heat. Allow the oatmeal to absorb all of the liquid (this should take about 15 minutes) prior to adding any supplements.

YIELD: 12 cups; 300 calories per cup

DAILY PORTION

Divide into two meals, or serve one-half the daily portion per day with one-half the normal amount of dry food.

10-POUND DOG	20-POUND DOG	40-POUND DOG	60-POUND DOG	80-POUND DOG
¾ to 1¼ cups	1½ to 2 cups	2⅔ to 3⅓ cups	3½ to 4½ cups	4½ to 5⅔ cups

BEEF AND BULGUR

With just a few minutes of cooking time and 20 minutes to sit off the heat, this is an incredibly easy meal to prepare.

2 tablespoons canola or olive oil

1½ pounds lean ground beef (85% lean)

2 medium zucchini, finely chopped

½ cup finely chopped red bell pepper

¼ teaspoon garlic powder

Heat the oil in a large Dutch oven over medium-high heat and add the ground beef, zucchini, bell pepper, and garlic powder.

Cook for 8 minutes, stirring frequently to break up the meat and to ensure all the meat is evenly browned.

3½ cups bulgur wheat

1 teaspoon dried oregano

Add the bulgur and oregano to the pot. Toss and cook until the bulgur is lightly toasted, about 3 minutes, stirring frequently.

6 cups water

1 (14-ounce) can diced tomatoes

Stir in the water and tomatoes. Bring to a simmer, then turn off the heat, cover, and allow to sit for 20 minutes, or until all of the liquid is absorbed. Allow the stew to cool prior to mixing in any supplements.

YIELD: 12 cups; 300 calories per cup

DAILY PORTION

Divide into two meals, or serve one-half the daily portion per day with one-half the normal amount of dry food.

10-POUND DOG	20-POUND DOG	40-POUND DOG	60-POUND DOG	80-POUND DOG
¾ to 1¼ cups	1½ to 2 cups	2⅔ to 3⅓ cups	3½ to 4½ cups	4½ to 5⅔ cups

BIRTHDAY BEEFCAKE (OR PUPCAKES)

When it's your dog's birthday and you want to do something special, give your dog meat, not wheat. Aim to please your pooch's palate with a Birthday Beefcake and he'll start wishing you celebrated seven dog birthdays a year. The frosting is made with mashed potatoes, so it looks the same and is easy to frost (enlist the kids to help) but avoids the calorie-dense cream cheese and sugar often found in pet frostings.

1 large egg 🐾 Preheat the oven to 350°F.

¼ cup chopped fresh parsley 🐾 Mix the egg with the parsley, then add the meat, carrot, and oats and mix well to combine.

⅓ pound ground beef (85% lean), turkey, or chicken

¼ cup shredded carrot

⅓ cup quick-cooking rolled oats

Pour the mixture into a 1-cup ovenproof baking dish or ramekin.

Bake for 45 minutes, then remove from the oven and allow to cool.

4 cups water 🐾 While the beefcake is cooking, bring the water to a boil, and add the potatoes. Decrease the heat to medium and cook for about 15 minutes, or until the potatoes can be pierced easily with a knife.

2 medium russet potatoes, cleaned of eyes and green spots, peeled and quartered

Drain the potatoes well and allow them to cool for 10 minutes.

2 tablespoons 2% milk 🐾 Add the milk and mash with a potato masher or handheld mixer until smooth, about 2 minutes. Do not overmix, or the potatoes will become gummy. If you have a few persistent chunks, your dog won't complain.

Remove the cake from the pan and place on a plate. Frost the cake with the potatoes and present to your dog with a song, but without the candles.

🐾 **YIELD:** 1 cake; 900 calories

PORTION FOR 1 MEAL				
10-POUND DOG	**20-POUND DOG**	**40-POUND DOG**	**60-POUND DOG**	**80-POUND DOG**
⅙ cake	¼ cake	½ cake	⅔ cake	1 cake

Your best friend enjoys eye rubs.

HEARTY BEEF

As an occasional meal this is a meaty treat, but it's even better when used to dress up boring dry kibble. The combination of meats brings together the best qualities of each type of meat. Beef heart is an inexpensive method of incorporating lean meat into your dog's diet and provides a good balance to the nutrients found in ground beef. It's a combination dogs love; it's good for them, and it's easy on your wallet.

Because this is mainly meat, it contains a high amount of phosphorus, which needs to be balanced out with calcium, so don't forget the eggshell supplement! If you're adding Supplement Stew (page 14), which contains Eggshell Powder already, the Eggshell Powder below can be omitted.

2 pounds ground beef (85% lean)	Add the ground beef, rosemary, and garlic powder to a large Dutch oven and heat over medium-high heat. Cook for 5 minutes, or until the beef begins to release juice and fat.
1 tablespoon fresh rosemary, chopped	
½ teaspoon garlic powder	
3 pounds beef heart (see Note)	Cut the beef heart into ½- to 1-inch cubes, then place it in a food processor and pulse for 10 seconds.
	Add the beef heart to the Dutch oven, and stir to combine.
¼ pound beef liver, chopped (see Note)	Stir in the beef liver and cook for 10 to 15 minutes, stirring 3 to 4 times throughout the cooking process, until all the meat is evenly browned.
2½ teaspoons Eggshell Powder (page 15)	Remove from the heat, stir in the Eggshell Powder, and allow the stew to cool prior to adding any supplements.
	YIELD: 11 cups; 330 calories per cup

NOTE: You'll need coarsely ground beef heart for this recipe, but it's not typically sold that way. Instead of cutting and processing the beef heart yourself, you could try asking your butcher to have it ground as "coarse ground."

When cutting beef liver, be aware that it is slippery and difficult to cut with a knife. Make it easier by placing the liver on a cutting board and snipping at it with kitchen shears.

DAILY PORTION

Divide into two meals, or serve one-half the daily portion per day with one-half the normal amount of dry food.
If your dog is not used to eating a large quantity of real meat, start out with one-quarter of the applicable amount below and slowly work your way to a larger serving size.

10-POUND DOG	20-POUND DOG	40-POUND DOG	60-POUND DOG	80-POUND DOG
⅔ to 1 cup	1¼ to 1⅔ cups	2⅓ to 3 cups	3¼ to 4 cups	4 to 5 cups

BEEF AND MAC
(WITH JUST A BIT OF CHEESE)

The secret to the macaroni and cheese that I serve at the dinner table is roasted butternut squash; I dice it, toss it with a couple tablespoons of olive oil, and roast it at 400°F for 25 minutes. The squash adds creaminess to the mac and cheese, which allows me to cut down the cheese by about one-third. Try this tip in your own mac and cheese recipe and you can utilize many of the same ingredients and most of the leftover produce to make a meal for your dog.

8 cups water

Bring the water to a boil in a large pot over high heat.

1 pound ground beef (85% lean)

3 cups peeled and cubed butternut squash (1-inch cubes)

¼ teaspoon garlic powder

Add the ground beef, butternut squash, and garlic powder and allow the pot to return to a boil.

1 pound dried macaroni

Add the macaroni, decrease the heat, and continue simmering for 16 minutes, or until the pasta and squash are both soft. (Pasta should be cooked for at least 2 to 3 minutes longer than package directions when preparing it for your pet.)

Drain the contents of the pot. (The reserved cooking liquid can be used in place of other stocks in cookie recipes. Store cooking liquids in the refrigerator for up to 4 days or in the freezer for up to 2 months.)

2 cups panko bread crumbs

½ cup lightly packed grated cheddar cheese

¼ cup chopped fresh parsley

Return the drained ingredients to the pot over medium heat. Add the bread crumbs, cheese, and parsley and toss all the ingredients to combine.

Remove from the heat and allow the mac and cheese to cool prior to mixing in any supplements.

YIELD: 14 cups; 260 calories per cup

DAILY PORTION

Divide into two meals, or serve one-half the daily portion per day with one-half the normal amount of dry food.

10-POUND DOG	20-POUND DOG	40-POUND DOG	60-POUND DOG	80-POUND DOG
1 to 1⅓ cups	1⅔ to 2⅓ cups	3 to 3¾ cups	4 to 5¼ cups	5 to 6⅓ cups

MUTT LOAF

Take off your rings, because the best way to mix any good meat loaf is with your hands. Like a friendly mutt, this meat loaf is a blend of different things. In this case, it's healthy, tasty ingredients that are easy to prepare.

Preheat the oven to 350°F.

3 medium russet potatoes, cleaned of eyes and green spots and grated

2 medium carrots, grated

Combine the potatoes and carrots in a large mixing bowl.

1 (15-ounce) can kidney beans, rinsed and drained

4 large eggs

1 teaspoon fresh rosemary, minced

¼ teaspoon garlic powder

In a food processor, combine the kidney beans, eggs, rosemary, and garlic powder. Process with 6 to 8 pulses, until the kidney beans are well chopped.

Combine the egg and bean mixture with the potatoes and carrots.

2¼ pounds ground beef (85% lean)

Add the beef and mix thoroughly to combine. Divide the mixture evenly between two 5 by 9-inch loaf pans and bake for 1 hour 10 minutes, or until the loaves reach 155°F when tested in the center with a meat thermometer.

Remove from the heat and allow the meat loaves to cool. To add supplement stew to this recipe, divide into equal portions and spread over the top of each loaf.

YIELD: 11 cups; 330 calories per cup

DAILY PORTION

Divide into two meals, or serve one-half the daily portion per day with one-half the normal amount of dry food.

10-POUND DOG	20-POUND DOG	40-POUND DOG	60-POUND DOG	80-POUND DOG
⅔ to 1 cup	1¼ to 1⅔ cups	2⅓ to 3 cups	3¼ to 4 cups	4 to 5 cups

BEEF AND POTATOES

Technically, this stovetop recipe should be called Potatoes and Beef because the potatoes outweigh the beef. However, when you mix this together, the potatoes will soak up all the juices from the beef and take on a meaty taste themselves. If you could ask your dog what this dish should be called, it's pretty likely that he'd call it Beef and Potatoes.

8 cups water	In a large stockpot, bring the water to a boil over high heat.
9 medium russet potatoes (about 3 pounds), cleaned of eyes and green spots	Cut the potatoes into ½-inch cubes. Add the potatoes to the boiling water and decrease the heat to medium. Simmer for 20 to 25 minutes with the lid slightly askew, until the potatoes are easily pierced with a fork. Drain the potatoes and set aside.
1 (10-ounce) package frozen green beans, thawed and coarsely chopped	In a food processor, pulse the green beans until finely chopped.
2½ pounds ground beef (85% lean) **1 tablespoon fresh rosemary, finely chopped** **¼ teaspoon garlic powder**	Add the beef, green beans, rosemary, and garlic powder to the pot that was used to cook the potatoes and cook over medium-high heat for 12 to 15 minutes, until the beef is browned. Stir frequently to break up the meat into smaller bites. Remove the beef mixture from the heat, stir in the potatoes, and allow to cool prior to mixing in any supplements.

YIELD: 12 cups; 300 calories per cup

DAILY PORTION

Divide into two meals, or serve one-half the daily portion per day with one-half the normal amount of dry food.

10-POUND DOG	20-POUND DOG	40-POUND DOG	60-POUND DOG	80-POUND DOG
⅔ to 1¼ cups	1½ to 2 cups	2⅔ to 3⅓ cups	3½ to 4½ cups	4½ to 5⅔ cups

HAMBURGER (AND MORE) PATTIES

Everyone loves a good hamburger, including your dog. By adding oats and some vegetables, these patties become lower in fat and even more nutritious. Plus, cooking these patties low and slow helps to prevent grease splatters and allows the oats time to absorb all the moisture, making them easier to digest. Neither man nor dog should try to live by hamburgers alone, but as an occasional treat they sure do taste good. This recipe makes half as much food as the other meal recipes; it's recommended that this make up no more than one-third of your dog's total diet since it's both a treat and a meal food in one.

1 large egg — In a large bowl, beat the egg with a fork.

1 cup quick-cooking rolled oats

1 pound ground beef (85% lean)

1 medium zucchini, grated

1 medium carrot, grated

¼ cup finely chopped fresh parsley

Add all of the remaining ingredients to the bowl and mix thoroughly.

Divide into eight portions. Gently roll one portion between your palms to form a ball. Press the ball into a patty ¾ inch thick and 3½ inches in diameter. Repeat with each of the remaining portions, layering them lightly on a plate.

Cook the patties 2 to 3 at a time in a nonstick skillet over medium heat for 6 minutes per side. When done cooking, transfer to a second, clean plate or a storage container.

To serve, allow to cool to slightly above room temperature, then crumble over dry food.

YIELD: 8 patties; 225 calories per patty

DAILY PORTION

Serve this amount per day with two-thirds the normal amount of dry food.

10-POUND DOG	20-POUND DOG	40-POUND DOG	60-POUND DOG	80-POUND DOG
½ patty plus dry food	¾ patty plus dry food	1⅓ patties plus dry food	1½ patties plus dry food	2 patties plus dry food

TINY TUNA NOODLE CASSEROLE

Here's a takeoff on a childhood classic that has a generous offering of cheese and a simple preparation that makes this a nice special-occasion treat. This recipe is sized so that you can siphon off a few ingredients when making your own tuna noodle casserole. Just be sure that your dog deserves his cheese by eating his peas.

5 cups water	Bring the water to a boil in a medium stockpot over high heat.
2 cups dried egg noodles ¼ cup frozen peas	Add the noodles and peas to the boiling water and allow the water to return to a boil. Cook for 10 minutes, until the noodles are very tender.
	Drain the noodles and peas, discarding the cooking liquid, and add the noodles and peas to a medium bowl.
1 (6-ounce) can water-packed tuna, drained	Add the tuna, yogurt, cheese, and bread crumbs to the bowl and gently toss to mix thoroughly.
¼ cup non-fat plain yogurt ¼ cup grated cheddar cheese	Allow the casserole to cool to slightly above room temperature before serving.
¼ cup panko bread crumbs	**YIELD:** 3 cups; 300 calories per cup

DAILY PORTION

Divide into two meals, or serve one-half the daily portion per day with one-half the normal amount of dry food.

10-POUND DOG	20-POUND DOG	40-POUND DOG	60-POUND DOG	80-POUND DOG
1 cup	1⅔ cups	3 cups	3 cups plus one-quarter regular food	3 cups plus one-third regular food

LAMB MUFFINS

A couple of times a year, I treat myself to some lamb chops. While the chops are cooking, the dogs all gather around while trying to figure out the source of that delicious smell. Here's a way to share a special-occasion treat with your dog. Because lamb is high in fat, it's best to combine this with half of your dog's regular food. Baking in a muffin tin helps to create individual serving sizes that you can easily store in the freezer.

Preheat the oven to 350°F.

½ cup water

4 large eggs

2 teaspoons fresh rosemary, finely chopped

¼ teaspoon garlic powder

Whisk the water, eggs, rosemary, and garlic powder in a large bowl.

1¼ pounds ground lamb

2¾ cups quick-cooking rolled oats

1 cup grated carrots or finely chopped green beans

Add the lamb, oats, and vegetables and stir to mix thoroughly.

Divide the mixture evenly in the wells of a 12-cup muffin tin and cook for 45 minutes.

Remove from the oven and allow to cool prior to serving.

Store in the refrigerator for up to 3 days or in the freezer for up to 2 months.

YIELD: 12 muffins; 300 calories per muffin

DAILY PORTION				
Serve this amount per day with one-half the normal amount of dry food.				
10-POUND DOG	**20-POUND DOG**	**40-POUND DOG**	**60-POUND DOG**	**80-POUND DOG**
½ muffin plus dry food	¾ muffin plus dry food	1½ muffins plus dry food	2 muffins plus dry food	2½ muffins plus dry food

SCOTCH BROTH

A taste of the Old World, this is a wonderful hearty stew made with lamb, vegetables, and barley. This is a more traditional method of making Scotch broth, but it can also be made by piling all the ingredients into a slow cooker, giving them a vigorous stir, and cooking on low for 5 to 7 hours. Nobody will blame you if you steal a bowl for yourself.

1 tablespoon olive oil

1½ pounds ground lamb

Heat the oil in a large Dutch oven over medium-high heat. Add the lamb and stir occasionally until the lamb is browned, about 8 minutes.

Stir in the garlic powder and allow to cook for 30 seconds.

¼ teaspoon garlic powder

8 cups water

2 cups pearl barley

2 medium carrots, cut into ½-inch dice

2 large turnips or rutabagas, cut into ½-inch dice

1 tablespoon fresh rosemary, finely chopped

Add the water, barley, carrots, turnips, and rosemary, then increase the heat to high.

Bring the soup to a boil, and then decrease the heat to low. Simmer until the lamb and barley are tender, about 1 hour.

2 cups finely chopped green beans

Stir in the green beans and simmer for 15 minutes longer.

Remove from the heat and allow the stew to cool prior to mixing in any supplements.

YIELD: 13 cups; about 280 calories per cup

DAILY PORTION				
Divide into two meals, or serve one-half the daily portion per day with one-half the normal amount of dry food.				
10-POUND DOG	**20-POUND DOG**	**40-POUND DOG**	**60-POUND DOG**	**80-POUND DOG**
1 to 1¼ cups	1⅔ to 2 cups	2¾ to 3½ cups	3¾ to 4⅔ cups	4⅔ to 5¾ cups

Your best friend travels first class.

PORK AND PENNE

Pork is often overlooked for feeding pets, but it's completely safe as long as it is cooked thoroughly. Pork is also easy on the pocketbook. A few quick pulses in the food processor turns pork shoulder into a wonderful sausage that pairs well with apples and penne.

8 cups water	Bring the water to a boil in a large stockpot. Add the penne and cook for 12 minutes, or until soft. (For your pet, pasta should be cooked at least 2 to 3 minutes longer than the package directions.)
1 pound dried penne	Drain the pasta, reserving 1 cup of the cooking water.
1½ pounds pork shoulder, trimmed of excess fat	Chop the pork in a food processor or cut it into ½-inch cubes for dogs less than 30 pounds or 1-inch cubes for dogs over 30 pounds. Heat the empty pot used for the pasta over medium-high heat and add the pork and reserved cooking liquid. Cook for 15 minutes, or until the meat is evenly cooked, stirring occasionally.
2 cups thawed frozen Swiss chard	Add the Swiss chard and cook for an additional 3 minutes, then remove the pot from the heat.
2 large red Gala apples, cored and cut into ½-inch dice	Add the pasta and apples to the pork mixture and stir well to combine. Allow the casserole to cool prior to mixing in any supplements.

YIELD: 13 cups; about 280 calories per cup

DAILY PORTION

Divide into two meals, or serve one-half the daily portion per day with one-half the normal amount of dry food.

10-POUND DOG	20-POUND DOG	40-POUND DOG	60-POUND DOG	80-POUND DOG
1 to 1¼ cups	1⅔ to 2 cups	2¾ to 3½ cups	3¾ to 4⅔ cups	4⅔ to 5¾ cups

RABBIT STEW

Some people might be a little uncomfortable about cooking rabbit, but your dog won't be uncomfortable about eating it. For most dogs, rabbit will be a new and exotic flavor. If your dog has sensitivities to common meats, try finding rabbit at a local grocery store specializing in Asian or Italian grocery products. It's usually inexpensive, and often in stock.

6 cups water

1 rabbit (about 2 pounds), cleaned

Bring the water and rabbit to a boil in a large stockpot over high heat. Decrease the heat to low and simmer for 1 hour.

Using tongs, remove the rabbit from the stockpot and place it in a colander set over a bowl. Return all drained liquids to the stockpot.

3 cups peeled and grated yams (about 1 pound)

3 cups quinoa

1 cup frozen peas

2 tablespoons olive oil

Add the yams, quinoa, peas, and oil to the cooking liquid and return to a boil.

Decrease the heat to low and simmer for 25 minutes, or until all the liquid is absorbed.

When the rabbit has cooled, remove the bones and coarsely chop the meat. Fold the meat into the quinoa mixture in the pot.

YIELD: 11 cups; 330 calories per cup

DAILY PORTION

Divide into two meals, or serve one-half the daily portion per day with one-half the normal amount of dry food.

10-POUND DOG	20-POUND DOG	40-POUND DOG	60-POUND DOG	80-POUND DOG
¾ to 1 cup	1½ to 1¾ cups	2⅓ to 3 cups	3¼ to 4 cups	4 to 5 cups

KIBBLE WORTH CHEWING

Commercial kibble lasts for only a few seconds on a dog's palate. This homemade recipe makes a chewy kibble that dogs will savor and enjoy. It's also a great kibble for dogs with sensitive mouths or as a treat recipe for families with large, well-behaved packs requiring treats in bulk.

Preheat the oven to 350°F.

Nonstick cooking spray

Spray a 12 by 18-inch rimmed baking sheet with nonstick cooking spray.

2 large eggs
1 cup water
¼ cup sunflower oil
1 (15-ounce) can solid-pack pumpkin puree
1 cup chopped fresh parsley

Whisk the eggs, water, sunflower oil, pumpkin, and parsley in a large bowl.

½ (10-ounce) package frozen spinach, thawed
1 pound ground beef (75% lean)

Add the spinach and ground beef to the egg mixture and stir to combine and break up the beef.

1½ cups rye flour
1½ cups quick-cooking rolled oats
½ cup nonfat instant powdered milk
¼ cup nutritional yeast

Add the flour, oats, powdered milk, and nutritional yeast and stir until combined.

Transfer the dough to the prepared baking sheet and press or roll to a ½-inch thickness.

Bake for 1 hour, then remove from the oven and allow to cool on the baking sheet. To create a firmer kibble, turn off the oven and allow the kibble to remain in the oven with the door closed for an additional hour.

When cooled, cut into 1-inch squares with a sharp knife.

YIELD: 11 cups; 330 calories per cup

DAILY PORTION

Divide into two meals, or serve one-half the daily portion per day with one-half the normal amount of dry food.

10-POUND DOG	20-POUND DOG	40-POUND DOG	60-POUND DOG	80-POUND DOG
⅔ to 1 cup	1⅓ to 1⅔ cups	2⅓ to 3 cups	3⅓ to 4 cups	4 to 5 cups

FEEDING GROWING PUPPIES

It takes a lot to grow up big and strong, and puppies are no exception to this rule. Feeding high-quality food will help build a strong foundation for your puppy's entire life. The weight of a puppy can double in a short period of time, and a lot of that will go directly to building muscle. Your puppy will need twice the amount of protein needed by an adult dog in his diet, and it should come from lean sources of meat. In comparison with other animals, puppies are born with low amounts of minerals in their skeletons. In the first year of life, your puppy requires two to three times as much of most minerals in his diet than his adult counterparts. Vitamins, in comparison, only need to be supplied in slightly larger quantities than for full-grown dogs.

The growth of a large-breed puppy needs to be slowly encouraged over 18 months to 2 years. While most vitamins and minerals are supplied in the same amount as for other breeds of puppies, those that help build a strong skeletal system must be provided in controlled amounts to prevent overly rapid growth. Throughout their long puppyhood, large-breed dogs should be kept lean, without being too thin.

Although puppies have those cute, pudgy bodies that are nice to cuddle with, maintaining an appropriate weight is important to reduce stress on their developing bodies and prevent obesity later in life. After they are about two months old, puppies should begin to develop a lean body with a slight covering of fat over the ribs, just like adults.

To determine how much food to feed your puppy, weigh your puppy at the beginning of each month and do a quick check of his ribs using the guidelines on page 22. For the following recipe for Powerful Puppy Food, the average amount that should be fed per day based upon your dog's current weight and age is estimated in the next table. Your puppy may need a little more or less depending on his breed, body type, and the amount of exercise he gets each day.

2 TO 3 MONTHS

WEIGHT	DAILY PORTION*	NOTES
1 pound	½ cup	At 2 months, a small-breed dog weighs an average of 31% of his adult weight; larger breeds weigh an average of 21% of their adult weight.
2 pounds	½ to 1 cup	
4 pounds	1 cup	At 3 months, a small-breed dog weighs an average of 45% of his adult weight; larger breeds weigh an average of 36% of their adult weight.
6 pounds	1 to 1½ cups	
8 pounds	1½ to 2 cups	
10 pounds	1½ to 2½ cups	Puppies should be weaned between 6 and 8 weeks. Feed solid foods in three or four meals.
12 pounds	2 to 3½ cups	
15 pounds	3 to 3½ cups	At 8 weeks, a puppy has completed his largest growth phase and his coordination has vastly improved. He is ready for his vaccinations now that he is no longer supported by his mother's milk.
18 pounds	3½ to 4½ cups	
20 pounds	4 cups	
25 pounds	5 cups	Teething starts in the third month; have plenty of toys available.
30 pounds	6½ cups	
35 pounds	7½ cups	

4 TO 6 MONTHS

WEIGHT	DAILY PORTION*	NOTES
1 pound	½ cup	At 4 months, a small-breed dog weighs an average of 56% of his adult weight; larger breeds weigh an average of 46% of their adult weight.
2 pounds	½ to 1 cup	
4 pounds	1 cup	At 5 months, a small-breed dog weighs an average of 64% of his adult weight; larger breeds weigh an average of 54% of their adult weight.
6 pounds	1 to 1½ cups	
8 pounds	1½ to 2 cups	
10 pounds	1½ to 2½ cups	At 6 months, a small-breed dog weighs an average of 69% of his adult weight; larger breeds weigh an average of 59% of their adult weight.
12 pounds	2 to 3½ cups	
15 pounds	3 to 3½ cups	Zinc and copper are required at higher levels during this phase of growth.
18 pounds	3½ to 4½ cups	
20 pounds	4 cups	Many dogs begin to exhibit a second fear stage around the sixth month. Encourage him rather than console him to help him grow into a big, brave dog.
25 pounds	5 cups	
30 pounds	6½ cups	
35 pounds	7½ cups	
45 pounds	5½ to 8 cups	This is a good period to begin training and extend socialization outside of the home.
50 pounds	6 to 7 cups	
55 pounds	6½ to 8 cups	
60 pounds	7 cups	
65 pounds	8 cups	

7 TO 9 MONTHS

WEIGHT	DAILY PORTION*	NOTES
1 pound	½ cup	At 7 months, a small-breed dog weighs an average of 73% of his adult weight; larger breeds weigh an average of 63% of their adult weight.
2 pounds	½ cup	
5 pounds	1 cup	At 8 months, a small-breed dog weighs an average of 76% of his adult weight; larger breeds weigh an average of 66% of their adult weight.
8 pounds	1 to 1½ cups	
10 pounds	1 to 1½ cups	
12 pounds	1½ to 2 cups	At 9 months, a small-breed dog weighs an average of 80% of his adult weight; larger breeds weigh an average of 70% of their adult weight.
15 pounds	2 cups	
18 pounds	2 to 2½ cups	Permanent teeth are still settling into your dog's jawbone, so remember to keep a variety of soft and hard toys available.
20 pounds	2½ cups	
25 pounds	3 cups	With a puppy out of his rebellious teenage period, this is a good time to introduce more advanced training. Try occasionally feeding your puppy one-quarter of a meal in training, and the remainder in the bowl.
30 pounds	3½ cups	
35 pounds	3½ to 4½ cups	
40 pounds	4½ to 5 cups	Daily portions can now be divided into two servings per day.
45 pounds	5 cups	
50 pounds	5½ cups	
55 pounds	5½ to 6 cups	
60 pounds	6 to 6½ cups	
65 pounds	6½ to 7 cups	
70 pounds	7 to 8 cups	
75 pounds	7 to 8 cups	
80 pounds	8 cups	

10 TO 12 MONTHS

WEIGHT	DAILY PORTION*	NOTES
1 pounds	½ cup	At 10 months, a small-breed dog weighs an average of 84% of his adult weight; larger breeds weigh an average of 75% of their adult weight.
2 pounds	½ cup	
4 pounds	½ to 1 cup	At 11 months, a small-breed dog weighs an average of 87% of his adult weight; larger breeds weigh an average of 78% of their adult weight.
6 pounds	1 cup	
8 pounds	1 cup	
10 pounds	1½ cups	At 12 months, a small-breed dog weighs an average of 91% of his adult weight; larger breeds weigh an average of 82% of their adult weight.
12 pounds	1½ to 2 cups	
15 pounds	2 cups	Most dogs will reach their adult height in this stage, but will continue to fill out. By now, dogs should have lost their cute puppy pudginess and resemble the standard for their breed. Check your pup's body condition and adjust feeding size as necessary.
18 pounds	2 cups	
20 pounds	2½ cups	
25 pounds	2½ to 3 cups	
30 pounds	3½ cups	
35 pounds	4 cups	
40 pounds	4 cups	
45 pounds	4½ to 5 cups	
50 pounds	5 to 5½ cups	
55 pounds	5½ to 6 cups	
60 pounds	6 cups	
65 pounds	6½ to 7 cups	
70 pounds	7 cups	
75 pounds	7½ cups	
80 pounds	7½ to 8 cups	
85 pounds	8 to 8½ cups	
90 pounds	8½ cups	
95 pounds	9 cups	

* Daily Portion is given for an average dog eating the Powerful Puppy Food recipe (page 131). Your dog may need +/-25% of the stated amount depending on breed, activity level, and body condition.

It takes a large amount of food each day to turn a puppy into a healthy adult dog. For the first 6 months of a puppy's life, divide the amount above into three to four meals per day. After 6 months, puppies can be fed twice a day.

Your best friend has a word for cookie.

POWERFUL PUPPY FOOD

Puppies are naturally curious about food, and will attempt to eat almost anything. This recipe provides the opportunity for you to instill a love of fruits and vegetables that will endure through adulthood. As you prepare each batch, vary the vegetables that you use—carrots, peas, spinach, apples, bananas, plums, lettuce, or any other fruits and vegetables listed on pages 29 through 32. Try to use at least two different fruits and vegetables in each batch.

2 cups mixed chopped fruits and vegetables

2 pounds boneless, skinless chicken thighs, diced into ½-inch cubes

2½ cups long-grain brown rice

7 cups water

¼ cup canola oil

1 (3.5-ounce) can sardines, packed in tomato sauce

Add the fruits and vegetables, chicken, rice, water, oil, and sardines to the pot of a 6-quart slow cooker and stir well to combine.

Set on low heat and cook for 6 hours, or until the rice is very tender and has absorbed all of the liquid.

1¼ teaspoons potassium chloride

⅔ cup Supplement Stew (page 14)

Turn off the cooker and allow the mixture to sit for 20 minutes. When the mixture has cooled slightly, stir in the potassium chloride and the Supplement Stew.

YIELD: 15 cups; 280 calories per cup

WARM-NOSE MEALS FOR AILING DOGS

ALLERGIES
Lamb, Millet, and Yams for Allergies

ARTHRITIS
Arthritis-Relieving Mackerel and Millet
Arthritis-Relieving Beef and Sweet Potato

CANCER
Cancer-Fighting Split-Pea Soup
Cancer-Fighting Turkey

DIABETES
Turkey and Barley for Diabetics

GASTROINTESTINAL DISEASES
Get-Well-Soon Congee
Sensitive-Stomach Rice and Egg
Sensitive-Stomach Chicken and Rice

HEART DISEASE
Healthy-Heart Beef and Yams
Healthy-Heart Chicken and Rice

KIDNEY (RENAL) DISEASE
Healthy-Kidney Potatoes and Beef
Healthy-Kidney Rice with Eggs

LIVER DISEASE
Liver Diet

WEIGHT LOSS

Chicken noodle soup is the age-old go-to for the common cold, not just because it helps to open nasal passages or because it tastes good, but also because homemade food says, "I love you." Just like Mom's chicken noodle, the foods in this chapter can help to alleviate symptoms and assist in healing even when they aren't necessarily a full cure. It is important to find the right combinations of foods that will assist healing and to follow any protocols recommended by your veterinarian.

I am the first person to admit that I am not a veterinarian, so I never diagnose or prescribe particular therapies. However, I know firsthand how difficult it can be for a person to watch a dog refuse to eat or to endure the agony of a pet's illness. When your best friend is sick, it's not just hard on your dog, it's also hard on you. An Internet search will present thousands of recommendations for any ailment. I'd rather see you go for a walk or sit down while watching TV to give your dog a good massage than spend hours on the Internet and reading books. This chapter is written to assist you in discussions with your own veterinarian and to provide you with reasonable, fact-based choices to use in conjunction with recommendations by professionals.

All of the recipes in this section have been developed from information written explicitly for veterinarians or by veterinarians themselves. When beginning any new meal plan for an ailing dog, you should first consult with your veterinarian. If your veterinarian suggests a commercial food, take a look at the ingredients very carefully, and don't be afraid to ask questions about the merits of the primary ingredients. Many of the veterinary prescription formulas are heavily corn-based and probably not the best source of nutrients for a sick dog. It's worth repeating: "Good nutrition is the key component of good health," which doesn't simply mean meeting a dog's vitamin and mineral requirements. It's also important to provide food that is appealing, wholesome, and based upon the freshest, most appropriate ingredients possible.

For each of the ailments included in this chapter, an overview of nutritional concerns is provided to assist your conversation with your veterinarian. It should be noted that the information is based on thorough research using professional resources. When your pet is seriously ill, take the matter seriously. Base your own research on the sources listed in the resources section at the end of the book and on discussions with your veterinarian rather than well-intentioned but often uninformed blogs, Web sites, and hand-me-down suggestions.

The majority of these recipes are prepared using a slow cooker because it both intensifies the flavors for your dog and gives you more time to spend with your dog. A sick dog doesn't always understand why he feels so crummy. However, when you provide your attention, some massages, exercise, and a warm bowl of chow, he will understand just how much you care.

Your best friend has two left feet.

ALLERGIES

Scratch, scratch, scratch. Scratch, scratch, scratch. Scratch, scratch, scratch. A dog's scratching due to consistent skin irritation is annoying for both man and beast. We can ignore it at first, but as the scratching becomes more persistent, we start looking for a cause and a possible solution. Sometimes, however, we leap to the conclusion without preceding it with a careful enough look at the situation.

Allergies do exist, and dogs who are on one brand and one flavor of food for the majority of their life often begin to develop allergies to specific ingredients. There can, however, be another cause of persistent itching. The dogs who I've most often seen with skin conditions are Labrador Retrievers. Labs were bred in Newfoundland to assist fishermen and were aided in that task with their dense, water-repelling coat. It was the fish, so high in omega-3s, that the dogs were not only helping to catch but were also eating, that helped to develop that water-loving coat. When we take away fish from the diet, we take away the omega-3s. The skin condition often deteriorates to the point where itching begins.

Omega-3 fatty acids, especially those found in salmon oil, are readily metabolized and utilized by the skin, making supplementation with salmon oil a good place to start when your dog is itching. You might also try mixing sardines packed in olive oil into your dog's food to add both nutrition and an exciting treat to the dog bowl (see page 35 for feeding amounts). Results are visible within a couple of weeks, but it can take up to 12 weeks of supplementation to fully resolve.

If the problem is most likely a food allergy, it's best diagnosed in the office of a veterinarian or dermatologist, not in the living room. The veterinarian will look for other signs, such as ear infections, hot spots, higher than normal bowel movements, and skin conditions that exist year-round. With a few tests, food allergens can be discovered and eliminated from the diet. If the allergen is environmental, veterinarians can also advise how to manage the condition.

When dogs have food allergies, it's imperative to eliminate all sources of the allergen from the diet, including snacks. The go-to diet for allergy sufferers at the moment seems to be duck and potato. Lamb is another good choice, especially if your dog has not been eating lamb in the past, as are rabbit and venison, for the same reason. Once allergies to specific protein sources develop, it's likely that new foods will later become allergens as well. It's important not to rotate through meats too quickly, or you may run out of options. Keep some proteins in reserve for when you really need them. Recipes such as the Arthritis-Relieving Mackerel and Millet on page 139 and the Rabbit Stew on page 123 can be other suitable options if your veterinarian recommends switching to other protein sources.

LAMB, MILLET, AND YAMS FOR ALLERGIES

This recipe uses lamb, which is more widely available than duck or venison, and combines it with millet, a grain that is far removed from the wheat family and believed to rarely cause allergies. Millet is most often used as bird feed, but it is a good choice to include in dog food because it provides protein, fiber, B vitamins, and minerals like copper and zinc.

1 cup millet	Add the millet, lamb, yams, water, rosemary, and garlic powder to the pot of a 6-quart slow cooker and stir well to combine.
1 pound ground lamb	
1½ pounds yams, grated	Cook on low heat for 6 hours, or until the millet has absorbed all the water.
3 cups water	
1 teaspoon finely chopped fresh rosemary	
¼ teaspoon garlic powder	
2 tablespoons salmon oil	Turn off the cooker and allow the mixture to sit for 20 minutes. When the mixture has cooled slightly, stir in the salmon oil and any other supplements.

YIELD: 10 cups; 370 calories per cup

DAILY PORTION

Divide into two meals, or serve one-half the daily portion per day with one-half the normal amount of dry food.

10-POUND DOG	20-POUND DOG	40-POUND DOG	60-POUND DOG	80-POUND DOG
⅔ to 1 cup	1⅓ to 1⅔ cups	2 to 2⅔ cups	2¾ to 3⅔ cups	3½ to 4½

ARTHRITIS

As our dogs live longer, the incidence of arthritis increases. Osteoarthritis is the condition in which carti-lage slowly degenerates and joints become increasingly stiff, losing their range of motion. Although many things can cause osteoarthritis, excessive exercise and extra weight are two of the factors that put dogs at risk. Inflammation, such as in rheumatoid arthritis, involves the immune system going into overdrive, attacking joints, tissues, and organs.

Prostaglandins are fatty acids that act like hormones and have many responsibilities in the body, one of which is to increase or decrease inflammation. The quantity and composition of antioxidants, carbohy-drates, fats, vitamins, minerals, and anti-inflammatory compounds in food determine whether there will be an excess of inflammatory prostaglandins in the body. By creating a diet that balances inflammatory and anti-inflammatory foods, the amount of detrimental prostaglandins can be reduced or, at the very minimum, not increased.

In her book *The Inflammation-Free Diet Plan*, Monica Reinagel goes into detail about food choices and offers a wide variety of menus for people with ailments caused by inflammation. Based upon her information, I've created two recipes using foods that are appropriate for dogs, but here are a few general suggestions for feeding dogs who have arthritis:

- Members of the nightshade family—eggplant, peppers, potatoes, and tomatoes—should be avoided.
- Sweet potatoes, butternut squash, and pumpkin are beneficial, whereas yams are not.
- Salmon and salmon oil both have anti-inflammatory properties. Wild salmon has a stronger effect than farmed salmon.
- Carbohydrates that have a high glycemic index (meaning they are more readily converted to glucose in the body) tend to be more inflammatory. Whole grains are used in the following recipes, and while these also have some inflammatory properties, this effect can be minimized with the other ingredients.
- Eggs are moderately inflammatory, but other sources of protein like ground beef have almost a neutral effect.
- Glucosamine/chondroitin supplements, derived from shellfish, are often used to ease the symptoms of arthritis. When purchasing and administering glucosamine or chondroitin supplements, take careful notice of the dosage, because it often takes two or more pills to equal the advertised dosage. Discuss precise dosages with your veterinarian.
- Cetyl myristoleate is advertised all over the Internet as a beneficial supplement for arthritis sufferers. However, it's difficult to track down specific scientific research that validates those claims. Discuss with your veterinarian prior to adding this supplement to your treatment regimen.

ARTHRITIS-RELIEVING MACKEREL AND MILLET

This meal is quick to prepare, so it's not necessary to use a slow cooker. The tiny grain needs a bit of extra help to ensure it's soft enough for dogs to digest, so here the millet is cooked with more water than we'd use in our foods. The result is fluffy millet that will keep your pet full with a sizable low-calorie portion.

10 cups water	Bring the water and millet to a boil in a large stockpot over high heat.
2¾ cups millet	
3 cups Swiss chard, cut into thin strips	Add the Swiss chard and olive oil to the millet, and then decrease the heat to low. Simmer for 35 to 40 minutes, until all the liquid is absorbed.
¼ cup olive oil	Remove the mixture from the heat and allow it to cool.
2 (15-ounce) cans mackerel	Drain the mackerel and chop it finely. Remove any large bones.
1 cup canned solid-pack pumpkin puree	Add the mackerel, pumpkin, parsley, and glucosamine supplement to the millet mixture and stir to combine.
½ cup chopped fresh parsley	**YIELD:** 15 cups; 240 calories per cup
3,000 milligrams glucosamine tablets with chondroitin, crushed or pulsed in a food processor	

DAILY PORTION

Divide into two meals, or serve one-half the daily portion per day with one-half the normal amount of dry food.

10-POUND DOG	20-POUND DOG	40-POUND DOG	60-POUND DOG	80-POUND DOG
1 to 1⅓ cups	2 to 2½ cups	3⅓ to 4¼ cups	4½ to 5⅔ cups	5½ to 7 cups

ARTHRITIS-RELIEVING BEEF AND SWEET POTATO

This provides a grain-free option for dogs with arthritis, with plenty of beefy flavor and the surprise of grated ginger to help ease their aching joints. Browning beef is quick and easy on the stovetop, and cooking the sweet potatoes in the microwave makes that step a cinch as well.

2 pounds ground beef (85% lean)

5 ounces frozen spinach, thawed

1½ cups water

1 teaspoon grated fresh ginger

In a large skillet over medium heat, cook the beef for 6 minutes. Add the spinach, ½ cup of the water, and ginger and cook for 6 minutes longer, stirring occasionally to break up the beef.

Remove from the heat and allow the beef mixture to cool.

3 pounds sweet potatoes, cleaned and cut into 1-inch cubes

Combine the sweet potatoes and the remaining 1 cup of water in a microwave-safe dish and cook on high power for 7 minutes. Stir the potatoes and cook on high for an additional 7 minutes.

3 tablespoons salmon oil

¼ cup chopped fresh parsley

3,000 milligrams glucosamine tablets with chondroitin, crushed or pulsed in a food processor

Allow the potato mixture to cool, and then combine it with the beef mixture, salmon oil, parsley, and glucosamine supplement in a large bowl.

YIELD: 12 cups; 295 calories per cup

DAILY PORTION

Divide into two meals, or serve one-half the daily portion per day with one-half the normal amount of dry food.

10-POUND DOG	20-POUND DOG	40-POUND DOG	60-POUND DOG	80-POUND DOG
⅔ to 1¼ cups	1½ to 2 cups	2⅔ to 3⅓ cups	3½ to 4½ cups	4½ to 5⅔ cups

Your best friend strikes a good bargain.

CANCER

I know firsthand how hard it is to hear the word *cancer* while sitting in the veterinarian's office. Half of our dogs will develop cancer; the reasons are unknown but the effects can be devastating. A group of cells in a dog's body can suddenly start multiplying at an uncontrolled rate, causing a lump or invading other parts of the body. Sudden weight loss, lethargy, and loss of appetite are subtle signs that often appear in the early stages of cancer. Early diagnosis can greatly improve the success of treatment, which is why any unusual symptoms your dog exhibits should be checked with your veterinarian. Combining an oncologist's treatment with appropriate nutrition will give your dog a fighting chance.

Dogs often begin to lose weight and muscle mass even while eating enough food because cancer cells are greedy and divert the nutrition in food to promote their own rapid growth. Carbohydrates, especially simple carbohydrates like sugars, are the cancer cell's preferred source of energy because they can be easily used to further the cancer's growth. Limiting the supply of simple carbohydrates in the diet cuts off cancer's energy supply. Other cells in the body can utilize fats for energy, making a high-fat, low-carbohydrate diet the best choice for dogs with cancer.

The metabolism of proteins, both in the diet and in the body itself, is also disrupted by cancer. Providing a high-protein diet helps dogs maintain healthy muscle tissue despite the effects of cancer. Arginine is not usually considered an essential amino acid for dogs because they can normally synthesize it in their kidneys. In the body, arginine has powerful effects on T-cell function and the immune system. Therefore, the following diets have more than 400 percent of the recommended daily amount of arginine to help a dog fight back against cancer.

Antioxidants are an important part of helping the body control free radicals and bolstering the immune system. Some of the most common antioxidants play a large role in fighting cancer:

- Vitamin A is a retinoid, a class of chemical compounds that help to control the growth of cancer. Liver, broccoli, carrots, sweet potatoes, and other vegetables are all high in vitamin A.
- Vitamin C not only helps maintain healthy cells, it is also believed to break down the cancer's resistance to drug therapy.
- Vitamin E, found in wheat germ oil, inhibits cancer growth.
- Selenium, found in the Supplement Stew's Brazil nuts, helps prevent tumors from developing and reduces the toxicity of chemotherapy in cooperation with vitamins A and E.

If possible, use organic produce and meat to prevent additional cancer-causing chemicals from being introduced to the body while your pet is struggling with cancer.

CANCER-FIGHTING SPLIT-PEA SOUP

I liked to have at least one of Jackson's meals each day be grain free. Using a modest portion of split peas will add protein and just enough complex carbohydrates to give your dog some energy. This recipe provides a healthy portion of chicken, prompting an ailing dog to come back for another check to see if anything is left in the bowl. The vegetables, garlic, and rosemary provide antioxidants, vitamins, and minerals that will bolster your dog's immune system, and they smell pretty good cooking.

1 pound chicken gizzards

Chop the gizzards into 1-inch chunks, or process for 15 seconds in a food processor to grind the meat. Add the gizzards to the pot of a 6-quart slow cooker.

2 pounds boneless, skinless chicken thighs, cut into 1-inch cubes

Add all of the remaining ingredients to the slow cooker and give it a couple of quick stirs.

4 cups butternut squash, peeled and cut into ½-inch cubes or grated

Cook on low heat for 6 to 8 hours, until the split peas have softened.

1¼ cups split green peas

Turn off the cooker and allow the soup to cool prior to mixing in any supplements.

1 cup chopped broccoli

¼ cup chopped chicken livers

YIELD: 13 cups; about 400 calories per cup

½ cup olive or sunflower oil

5 cups water

2 tablespoons finely chopped fresh rosemary

¼ teaspoon garlic powder

DAILY PORTION

Divide into two meals, or serve one-half the daily portion per day with one-half the normal amount of dry food.

10-POUND DOG	20-POUND DOG	40-POUND DOG	60-POUND DOG	80-POUND DOG
⅔ to 1 cup	1¼ to 1½ cups	2 to 2½ cups	2⅔ to 3⅓ cups	3⅓ to 4¼ cups

Your best friend prefers hello to good-bye.

CANCER-FIGHTING TURKEY

This meal is mostly meat, giving a dog with cancer something worth fighting for. The wheat germ adds a natural source of vitamin E to strengthen your dog's immune system.

3 pounds ground turkey

4 cups diced yams

1 cup thawed frozen spinach

⅓ cup canola oil

1 tablespoon finely chopped fresh rosemary

¼ teaspoon garlic powder

Combine the turkey, yams, spinach, oil, rosemary, and garlic powder in the pot of a slow cooker.

Stir to combine, then cook on low heat for 6 to 8 hours.

Turn off the cooker and allow the stew to cool to room temperature.

2 medium red apples, any variety, cored and finely diced

¼ cup wheat germ

Add the apples, wheat germ, and any supplements to the turkey mixture and stir to mix well.

YIELD: 10 cups; about 360 calories per cup

DAILY PORTION

Divide into two meals, or serve one-half the daily portion per day with one-half the normal amount of dry food.

10-POUND DOG	20-POUND DOG	40-POUND DOG	60-POUND DOG	80-POUND DOG
⅔ to 1 cup	1⅓ to 1⅔ cups	2 to 2⅔ cups	3 to 3⅔ cups	3⅔ to 4⅔ cups

DIABETES

The pancreas produces insulin, which allows glucose, a sugar, to be used by the body's cells for energy. Dogs with diabetes have either an insufficient amount of insulin or the insulin is not effective enough to provide the cells with enough glucose. The cells start looking for other sources of energy and begin using the body's stores of protein, fat, and starches instead of glucose, which begins to build up in the body. The excess glucose can't be stored in the body, so it is processed by the kidneys and flushed out with lots of water, which is why pets with diabetes usually have excessive thirst and urination. Diabetes is usually noticed in adult dogs between the ages of 7 and 9, but it can affect dogs at any age.

Most diabetic dogs need to have their insulin levels managed through insulin injections, but proper nutrition and exercise are also important to prevent any sudden spikes in blood sugar levels. Overweight dogs have additional difficulty in maintaining consistent glucose levels and should be trimmed down with a combination of diet and exercise. Feeding schedules and amounts should be kept consistent, and in the case of diabetes, dogs should not be fed widely varying diets.

Here are a few guidelines for feeding your diabetic dog:

- Complex carbohydrates are much preferred because they digest more slowly than simple carbohydrates; and with a lower amount of sugars, like glucose, they are less likely to create a sudden spike in blood sugar levels. At least 50 percent of a dog's diet should come from complex carbohydrates.
- Fiber further slows the digestive process and the absorption of glucose as well as provides a little extra bulk to the diet without added calories, which will help dogs lose weight. Foods rich in complex carbohydrates also provide fiber, but the recipe in this section uses wheat bran to provide the 15 percent recommended by veterinarian nutritionists. Because wheat bran is an insoluble fiber, it won't absorb an excess amount of water; dogs are also less likely to have diarrhea with wheat bran than when fed high amounts of soluble fiber.
- For treats, try giving your dog vegetables such as carrots, or lean slices of meat, instead of cookies and biscuits.

TURKEY AND BARLEY FOR DIABETICS

The green beans, Swiss chard, cumin, and cinnamon in this recipe have all been shown to be beneficial in laboratory tests on rats and are often recommended for humans with diabetes. The red pepper provides a great source of vitamin C, which will aid in normalizing blood sugar levels and improving kidney function, as well as preventing cataracts. The wheat germ oil provides vitamin E, which will also help protect eye health. This meal has an added benefit of being low in fat to help dogs with diabetes trim down.

3 cups pearl barley

8 cups water

1½ pounds ground turkey

1 medium red bell pepper, seeded and finely chopped

½ cup finely chopped frozen green beans

½ cup Swiss chard

¼ cup wheat bran

½ teaspoon ground cumin

½ teaspoon ground cinnamon

2 teaspoons canola oil

Combine the barley, water, turkey, bell pepper, green beans, Swiss chard, wheat bran, cumin, cinnamon, and oil in the pot of a 6-quart slow cooker.

Stir well to break up the turkey and mix the ingredients.

Cook on low heat for 6 to 8 hours, until the barley has absorbed all the water.

Turn off the cooker and allow the stew to cool.

YIELD: 15 cups; 220 calories per cup

DAILY PORTION

Divide into two meals, or serve one-half the daily portion per day with one-half the normal amount of dry food.

10-POUND DOG	20-POUND DOG	40-POUND DOG	60-POUND DOG	80-POUND DOG
1¼ to 1½ cups	2 to 2½ cups	3⅓ to 4⅓ cups	4⅔ to 6 cups	6 to 7½ cups

GASTROINTESTINAL DISEASES

A dog's digestive plumbing may break down for any number of reasons, causing diarrhea, vomiting, loss of appetite, or abdominal discomfort. Dogs with chronic diarrhea or vomiting are a challenge to feed because few foods stay in place long enough for nutrients to be absorbed, and the cleanup isn't fun either. If your dog has severe digestive problems, it's best to consult with your veterinarian to diagnose the cause and determine any medical treatments, but the feeding regimen is often the same.

The objective for feeding dogs with colitis, gastritis, or pancreatitis is to provide nutrition without causing further upset and to make any changes gradually to ensure that your pet's condition is not aggravated by a sudden shift. While dogs with normal digestive systems can often eat a variety of foods with no issue, even slight changes can cause a dog with gastrointestinal diseases to have diarrhea or vomiting for days. Always make changes in baby steps.

The foods selected for these diets are extremely limited because they focus on high digestibility. Eggs are the best source of digestible protein and require fewer enzymes to be digested, so your dog will be able to absorb more nutrients with less effort. Chicken breasts are another good source of protein because they are low in fat and high in protein. For grains, rely on white rice, which when well cooked is highly digestible. If you notice your dog is not fully digesting the rice, add more water in the cooking process.

By reducing fat, the likelihood of intestinal inflammation and associated diarrhea can be decreased. However, dogs do need a small amount of fat, so oils are added, but in small amounts. Salmon oil helps reduce inflammation and provides vitamins A, D, and E. Another benefit is that salmon oil will help make the diet more palatable; after all, rice and chicken can get boring day after day. Although dogs normally can produce vitamin K in their intestines, a dog with a compromised system will need some additional support, so where needed, canola oil or corn oil is added, which will also help supply vitamin E.

Supplementation is necessary because digestive issues inhibit nutrient absorption, and even though rice, eggs, and chicken are great foods, they cannot supply everything your dog requires. Zinc and a salt substitute, potassium chloride, are added to help bolster the immune and digestive systems, as the amounts of these provided in the multivitamin are not sufficient.

- Feed smaller, more frequent meals. As noted earlier, feeding three to four times a day eases the workload on your dog's plumbing. Even if the meals are just a couple of hours apart, it helps.
- Steer clear of cheese, milk, yogurt, and cottage cheese even as occasional treats to prevent their lactose from aggravating your dog's digestive system. Instead, try the recipe for Sardine Croutons on page 53; these can be a great treat for your dog.
- An occasional addition of pumpkin puree may help ease diarrhea. Add in small amounts to prevent adding too much fiber to your dog's diet. You may also add 2 to 3 teaspoons of psyllium husk if your veterinarian suggests increasing the fiber content, which may help some of the meal be digested better in the small intestine. However, when a dog's condition is first being stabilized, the fiber content should be kept low.

GET-WELL-SOON CONGEE

When your dog is feeling ill or recovering from medical procedures, veterinarians suggest a light meal. Because a dog's stomach needs a gentle recovery, rice is a great start. A friend of mine once brought congee when I was sick during a business trip in Asia. She said her mom made it for her when she was sick as a child. It helped me, and it will provide nutrition to your dog while being sensitive to her condition.

For the first few meals, keep it simple. As your dog's condition improves and his appetite returns, include one of the additions that follow the recipe. When you feel confident that your dog is tolerating the new meals, combine with your dog's normal dry food for a day, feeding half congee and half dry food.

Because this meal is designed to get your dog back on its paws, the simplicity does not allow this meal to be nutritionally balanced and so it should only be used for short periods of time.

2 cups Chicken Stock (page 66)

2 cups water

1 cup medium-grain white rice

Additions:

1 cup diced chicken breast, boiled and drained, or ½ cup 85% lean ground beef, boiled and drained, or ½ cup low-fat cottage cheese

Bring the stock, water, and rice to a boil in a medium saucepan.

Decrease the heat to low and adjust the lid to allow steam to escape.

Simmer for 30 minutes, or until the rice is creamy and thick, stirring occasionally to prevent the rice from sticking. Allow to cool to room temperature prior to serving.

YIELD: 4 to 5 cups, depending on additions

ALLOWANCE PER MEAL

FIRST MEAL: ⅓ of your dog's normal meal size, as tolerated.

SECOND MEAL: ⅔ of your dog's normal meal size, as tolerated.

THIRD AND FOURTH MEALS: Combine with dry food, as tolerated.

SENSITIVE-STOMACH RICE AND EGG

Dogs with sensitive stomachs often need easy-to-digest foods that won't upset their stomach and provide a maximum amount of nutrition. Cooking the rice in plenty of water allows for the stomach to break it down easier and using the whites of the eggs provides more nutrition without the added fat that can cause problems.

8 cups water

4 cups medium-grain white rice

Combine the water and rice in a 4-quart saucepan and bring to a boil over medium-high heat.

Decrease the heat to low and simmer for 30 minutes, or until all the water is absorbed.

Remove from the heat and let the rice stand, covered, for 5 minutes.

12 large eggs

Separate 6 of the eggs, reserving the whites and discarding the yolks or reserving them for another purpose.

In a medium bowl, add the remaining 6 whole eggs to the egg whites and beat lightly with a whisk until the eggs are combined.

Heat a large nonstick skillet over medium-low heat.

These supplements should be included on any long-term diets, as they are tolerated.

Add the eggs and stir gently for 5 to 6 minutes, until the eggs are dry. Remove from the heat and allow the eggs to cool.

2 multivitamin tablets (One A Day Men's preferred)

1 (50-milligram) zinc tablet

2 tablespoons water

Combine the multivitamins, zinc, and water in a small bowl and let sit for 20 minutes. Stir to dissolve the multivitamins, breaking up with a spoon if necessary.

2 tablespoons salmon oil

2 tablespoons nutritional yeast

1 tablespoon Eggshell Powder (page 15)

Add the salmon oil, nutritional yeast, Eggshell Powder, and potassium chloride to the water mixture and stir to combine.

Mix the cooked eggs, rice, and supplement mixture in a large bowl and stir to combine.

½ teaspoon potassium chloride (salt substitute)

YIELD: 14 cups; 260 calories per cup

DAILY PORTION

Divide into two meals.

10-POUND DOG	20-POUND DOG	40-POUND DOG	60-POUND DOG	80-POUND DOG
1 to 1⅓ cups	1⅔ to 2⅓ cups	3 to 4 cups	4 to 5¼ cups	5 to 6½ cups

SENSITIVE-STOMACH CHICKEN AND RICE

Another high-quality protein source that can be used instead of eggs is chicken breast. Because chicken breasts are lean, they also help prevent stomach upset from too much fat. A little canola oil is added to ensure that your dog receives enough essential fatty acids.

1½ pounds boneless, skinless chicken breasts, cut into ½-inch dice

3½ cups medium-grain white rice

7 cups water

1 tablespoon canola oil

¼ teaspoon salt

Combine all of the ingredients in a 4-quart saucepan and bring to a boil over medium-high heat.

Decrease the heat to low and simmer for 25 minutes, or until all the water is absorbed.

Remove from the heat and let the rice mixture stand, covered, for 5 minutes. Allow to cool before serving.

YIELD: 13 cups; 275 calories per cup

DAILY PORTION

Divide into two meals.

10-POUND DOG	20-POUND DOG	40-POUND DOG	60-POUND DOG	80-POUND DOG
1 to 1¼ cups	1⅔ to 2¼ cups	2⅔ to 3⅔ cups	4 to 5¼ cups	5 to 6½ cups

HEART DISEASE

Although some heart diseases like heartworm disease can be resolved, most congenital, degenerative, and infectious heart diseases are chronic and will continue to develop once diagnosed. Circulation of the blood is the primary function of the heart. When the heart is diseased, a domino effect begins; the heart cannot pump blood throughout the body effectively, so the body begins to retain sodium, which forces the kidneys to retain water. All this is an attempt to ensure that each beat of the heart, although weaker, will push through a greater amount of blood. Unfortunately, fluid retention ends up straining the heart further and may compromise the function of the kidneys and liver.

Proper veterinary care and medication are essential, as is providing appropriate nutrition. Both the condition and some of the required treatments may cause a dog's appetite to suffer, preventing necessary nutrition from getting in to do its job. Normal commercial diets often contain 500 percent or more of the recommended daily allowance of sodium to make them more palatable. The commercial diets for dogs with heart disease reduce the amount of sodium and are often based more on grains than meat, so there's not much flavor to interest your dog in returning to the bowl. To make matters worse, when a dog does eat, increased urination flushes necessary proteins, vitamins, and minerals out of the body.

To complement veterinary care, a proper diet must help replenish nutrients and antioxidants in quantities sufficient enough to counter the body's inability to absorb and retain them effectively. Here are a few special concerns:

- Sodium should be reduced to correspond with the recommended daily allowance (.08 percent of the total dry matter weight) to help regulate fluid retention. In the recipes that follow, we'll add flavor using foods like liver instead of salt.
- L-carnitine, a protein, helps metabolize fats for energy. Although the kidneys normally synthesize the L-carnitine required from other proteins (methionine and lysine), when sufficient levels of vitamins and minerals (B_3, B_6, C, and iron) are present, the kidneys are plenty busy filtering all the fluid in the body, and vitamins and minerals are not being kept in reserve. Your veterinarian may suggest supplementation, but we can also supplement by using one of the best sources of L-carnitine: red meat (¼ pound of ground beef supplies more than 100 mg of L-carnitine).
- Potassium helps to maintain the body's balance of fluid and electrolytes. Low-sodium diets and the extra work of the kidneys often deplete potassium, so we'll use potatoes, spinach, and the salt substitute potassium chloride to bring levels back up.
- Magnesium is essential to every cell in the body to maintain the balance of vitamins and minerals, enable enzyme functions, and regulate the composition of bones. Spinach is a great food source here as well.
- B vitamins are water soluble and therefore often lost through urination, so we need to ensure an adequate supply is presented in the diet with foods like nutritional yeast, liver, and sardines.

- Balancing out nutritional needs is essential, so a vitamin supplement should be added after the food has been prepared. Including supplements as part of the process in making the food, rather than giving them as a daily occurrence, will be easier on both you and your pet.

- If your dog is overweight, reducing calories is also important. Excess weight causes the heart to pump blood through a lot of extra tissue and fat. When your dog trims down, each heartbeat becomes more effective. The chicken and rice meal is designed for dogs with a normal appetite who also need to lose a few pounds. If your dog is less than enthusiastic about the food bowl, the beef and yams meal will entice him and pack nutrition in as little volume as possible so that every bite will count.

- The body's use of water is troublesome, but with the proper diet and veterinary care, equilibrium can be achieved. Always be sure to have plenty of water available, preferably distilled or filtered to ensure purity. Tap water that is filtered through a water softener should not be used because of the sodium used in the filtration process.

- Many dogs have the unfortunate complication of both kidney disease and heart disease. If this is the case with your dog, follow the recipes for kidney disease instead.

HEALTHY-HEART BEEF AND YAMS

This is an easy meal to prepare while you're making your own dinner because it takes advantage of a slow cooker. To make cutting the beef liver easier, freeze it for an hour before you cut it; or if the liver is already frozen, let it defrost at room temperature for an hour before cutting.

2 pounds ground beef (85% lean)

¼ cup beef liver, cut into ½-inch pieces

2 pounds yams, cut into ½-inch pieces (about 7 cups)

1 cup thawed frozen spinach

2 tablespoons finely chopped fresh rosemary

¼ teaspoon garlic powder

1 cup water

2 tablespoons nutritional yeast

Stir the beef, liver, yams, spinach, rosemary, garlic powder, and water in the pot of a 6-quart slow cooker.

Simmer on low heat for 4 to 6 hours, until the yams are soft and the beef is cooked through.

Turn off the cooker, stir in the nutritional yeast, and allow the stew to cool to room temperature.

YIELD: 13 cups; 280 calories per cup

DAILY PORTION

Divide into two meals, or serve one-half the daily portion per day with one-half the normal amount of dry food.

10-POUND DOG	20-POUND DOG	40-POUND DOG	60-POUND DOG	80-POUND DOG
1 to 1¼ cups	1⅔ to 2 cups	2¾ to 3½ cups	3¾ to 4⅔ cups	4⅔ to 5¾ cups

HEALTHY-HEART CHICKEN AND RICE

Chicken heart is an inexpensive meat that is higher in copper, zinc, and important B vitamins than other cuts of chicken like thighs or breasts. Their lower sodium content makes them a heart-healthy choice, and the small size requires only a bit of chopping for smaller dogs. Brown rice is a much healthier choice than white rice because it retains the outer bran covering, making it higher in nutrients and fiber.

2 pounds chicken hearts, cut in half for dogs less than 30 pounds

¼ cup chopped chicken livers

2½ cups brown rice

6 cups water

2 medium zucchini, grated

2 tablespoons canola oil

1 teaspoon potassium chloride (salt substitute)

1 (3.5-ounce) can sardines, packed in tomato sauce

2 tablespoons nutritional yeast

Stir the chicken hearts, livers, rice, water, zucchini, oil, and potassium chloride in the pot of a 6-quart slow cooker.

Simmer on low heat for 4 to 6 hours, until all the liquid has been absorbed.

Remove from the heat and allow the stew to cool to room temperature. Stir in the sardines and nutritional yeast.

YIELD: 13 cups; 280 calories per cup

DAILY PORTION

Divide into two meals, or serve one-half the daily portion per day with one-half the normal amount of dry food.

10-POUND DOG	20-POUND DOG	40-POUND DOG	60-POUND DOG	80-POUND DOG
1 to 1¼ cups	1⅔ to 2 cups	2¾ to 3½ cups	3¾ to 4⅔ cups	4⅔ to 5¾ cups

KIDNEY (RENAL) DISEASE

The kidney acts as a filter to clean the blood and eliminate waste through the urine while also regulating the ratio of calcium and phosphorus in the blood. At the onset of kidney disease, toxins will at first be present in the blood, but not at dangerous levels. In the second stage of kidney disease, toxins will be building up but there will be no visible symptoms. Symptoms such as lethargy, increased thirst, frequent urination, and loss of appetite will begin to appear as dogs enter the third stage of kidney disease. In the third stage, only about one-third of kidney function remains. If kidney function continues to deteriorate to 25 percent of normal function, dogs enter renal failure. Because the kidneys do not regenerate, the primary goals of treatment are preserving kidney function and delaying further progression of the disease.

Kidney disease is best managed by following your veterinarian's guidelines specific to your dog. Adding a thoughtful approach to nutrition will also lighten the load on the kidneys. As kidney disease progresses, your dog will begin to drink heavily and often refuse food. Unfortunately, the commercial diets for dogs with kidney disease are often bland and fail to entice dogs to eat. In determining a diet for dogs with renal disease, the goal is to minimize the intake of nutrients that compromise renal function or that cause substantial difficulty for the kidneys to process, while also making the food appetizing. Here are a few key nutrients to be watchful of when feeding a dog with kidney disease:

- Phosphorus is utilized in the bones and to transfer energy to every cell of the body. In dogs with renal disease, phosphorus overstays its welcome instead of being eliminated in the urine. This buildup causes the kidneys to steal calcium from the body's bones in order to bring the amount of calcium and phosphorus in the blood back into balance. That's not good news for bones or the kidneys. Dry foods prepared for dogs with renal disease supply about 80 percent of the normal recommended amounts of phosphorus, and the diets here emulate that restriction.
- Protein is used throughout the body, but in order for it to do its work, it must first be broken down through digestion. When proteins are metabolized, they create toxic by-products that are usually processed through the kidneys. Feeding a higher-quality protein but in smaller quantities reduces demand on the kidneys, relieves hypertension, and lightly applies the brakes to the progression of renal disease.
- Sodium reduction assists in relieving hypertension, but enough sodium must be supplied to help bring water through the kidneys. The following diets supply slightly less than the recommended daily allowance.
- Magnesium is kept close to the normal recommended daily allowance to prevent calcium crystallization and formation of kidney stones.
- Potassium can be depleted with increased urination, so potassium is increased slightly above the RDA.

Your best friend is at the other end of the leash.

- The average commercial dry food may supply up to six times the nutritional requirement of vitamin D. For dogs with normal kidney function, this does not have any adverse effects. However, vitamin D is also a nephrotoxin, which means it can harm the nephrons that compose the kidneys and do the actual filtering work. The diets here provide an adequate, but not more restricted, amount of vitamin D.

- Fermentable fiber helps to shift some of the kidney's workload to the colon. Psyllium husk acts as a source of fermentable fiber.

- With your dog drinking extra water, water-soluble vitamins may be excreted before they are fully absorbed, so increased amounts of B vitamins and vitamin C are included in the following diets.

- Omega-6 and omega-3 fatty acids are believed to promote proper kidney function. Ordinarily the recommended ratio of omega-6 to omega-3 fatty acids is around 10 to 1. For dogs with kidney disease, increasing the amount of omega-3 to achieve a ratio of 5 to 1 is accomplished with the addition of salmon oil.

- Some dogs may suffer from zinc and iron deficiencies; consult with your veterinarian to see if these should be added to the Supplement Stew.

Enticing dogs to eat when sometimes they just don't feel like it can be difficult. A couple of recipes have been included that meet the preceding requirements and keep mealtime interesting. These diets are also low in calories per cup of food; if your dog enjoys eating, they can be great diets on their own. However, if your dog only nibbles, you may want to combine them with a commercial diet designed for dogs with kidney disease. The commercial diets are usually higher in calories per cup but lack flavor. Combining a home-cooked meal with a commercial diet will increase palatability and help your pet maintain a healthy weight.

Healthy-Kidney Potatoes and Beef

By mixing some reserved potato water with the beef, the flavor of the beef is spread around, even if there isn't much beef included. With the addition of fish oil, omega-3 fatty acids are increased, and the nutritional yeast adds a boost of B vitamins.

5 pounds potatoes, skin on, cleaned of eyes and green spots and quartered

Water to cover

Bring the potatoes and water to cover to a boil in a large pot over high heat. Decrease the heat to low and simmer for 15 to 20 minutes, until the potatoes are easily pierced with a fork.

Drain the potatoes in a colander, reserving ½ cup of the cooking liquid.

¾ pound ground beef (75% lean)

1 medium red bell pepper, seeded and diced

Add the reserved liquid, beef, and bell pepper to the pot used for the potatoes and cook over medium-low heat for 10 to 12 minutes, until the beef is browned. Stir occasionally to break up the beef.

1 cup minced fresh parsley

¼ cup nutritional yeast

¼ cup salmon oil

2 teaspoons psyllium husk

Remove the pot from the heat and allow to cool. Add the potatoes, parsley, yeast, salmon oil, and psyllium husk and stir to combine.

YIELD: 15 cups; 230 calories per cup

DAILY PORTION

Divide into two meals, or serve one-half the daily portion per day with one-half the normal amount of dry food.

10-POUND DOG	20-POUND DOG	40-POUND DOG	60-POUND DOG	80-POUND DOG
1 to 1½ cups	2 to 2½ cups	3⅓ to 4¼ cups	4½ to 5⅔ cups	5½ to 7 cups

HEALTHY-KIDNEY RICE WITH EGGS

Bring a picky eater back to the bowl with the taste of eggs, which are more exciting for your dog than boring old rice. This recipe has more calories per cup than the Healthy-Kidney Potatoes and Beef recipe on page 159; so if you're dog isn't eating much, this is a good choice to help keep her strength up.

3½ cups brown rice 🐾 Place the rice, water, and oil in a 2-quart saucepan with a lid.

9 cups water · Bring to a boil over high heat, stirring once or twice, and cover.

¼ cup canola oil · Decrease the heat to the lowest setting and simmer for 35 to 40 minutes, until tender. Do not remove the lid during the cooking process.

7 large eggs 🐾 Mix the eggs and parsley in a medium bowl. Heat a small frying pan over medium heat and add the egg mixture. Cook for 4 to 5 minutes, occasionally turning the eggs over, until they are set.

½ cup chopped fresh parsley

1 (3.5-ounce) can sardines, packed in tomato sauce 🐾 When the rice is done, remove from the heat and stir in the egg mixture, sardines, potassium chloride, and psyllium husk. Allow the mixture to cool prior to adding any supplements.

2 teaspoons potassium chloride (salt substitute)

🐾 **YIELD:** 12 cups; 300 calories per cup

2 teaspoons psyllium husk

DAILY PORTION

Serve this amount with one-half the normal amount of dry food.

10-POUND DOG	20-POUND DOG	40-POUND DOG	60-POUND DOG	80-POUND DOG
⅔ to 1¼ cups	1½ to 2 cups	2⅔ to 3⅓ cups	3½ to 4½ cups	4½ to 5⅔ cups

Your best friend is your softball coach.

LIVER DISEASE

The liver is one of the body's busiest organs, acting as a production facility, warehouse, and waste treatment plant all in one as it converts nutrients for use in the body, stores nutrients, and filters toxins produced by digestion and the body's normal functions. When any of these important functions are compromised by liver disease, the whole body can be affected, with the most prominent signs appearing as a lack of appetite, increased water consumption, weakness, depression, and/or grayish feces.

The liver has the most incredible regenerative abilities of any organ, but to heal, it must receive proper nutrition. Nutrients that stress the liver should be reduced, as should any nutrients that the liver stores in high concentrations. Supplying enough of each nutrient to assist the body in normal functioning, yet not creating chaos for the liver, is a delicate balancing act that requires attention to detail. Here are a few guidelines:

- Metabolizing animal proteins produces toxic ammonia. Because the liver is already having a hard time keeping up with the body's requirements, protein, particularly animal proteins, should be fed in lower quantities. The diet here provides 22 percent protein, with only one-third of that coming from animal sources.
- Carbohydrates and proteins should be easily digestible. The following recipe relies mainly on cottage cheese and rice.
- Sodium should be restricted, so it's best to start reading labels. The Friendship Dairies brand of cottage cheese offers a no-added-salt choice, but other low-sodium brands can also be used. Also look for chicken without added salt or preservatives.
- The liver stores the mineral copper and normally eliminates the excess with bile production. With reduced liver function, copper sticks around and starts to build up to toxic levels. This recipe includes copper in a slightly lower amount than the recommended daily allowance.
- Zinc is an important contributor to the liver's ability to metabolize nutrients, but it is often deficient in dogs with liver disease. Zinc helps to convert ammonia to a safer form, urea, which is less stressful to the liver. In addition, an increased amount of zinc in the diet reduces the amount of copper absorbed. Because zinc is such an important player, this diet doesn't just rely on the zinc in the multivitamin; it also calls for an additional amount to ensure your dog gets more than twice the recommended daily allowance.
- Vitamin A is also stored in the liver in great quantities (which is why chicken and beef liver are also so high in this vitamin). To prevent toxicity, dogs with liver disease should not receive carrots, pumpkin, spinach, Swiss chard, liver, or other foods high in vitamin A.
- Feeding a dog with liver disease more frequently (three or four smaller meals a day) can help the dog metabolize nutrients and reduce stress on the liver.

LIVER DIET

This diet is specifically formulated for dogs with liver disease and includes supplements in proportions to aid the liver. The Supplement Stew recipe should not be added or used in substitution.

5 cups water

Bring the water to a boil in a large pot.

1 pound boneless, skinless chicken thighs, cut into ½-inch cubes

2 cups medium-grain white rice

1 red bell pepper, seeded and cut into ½-inch pieces or grated

Add the chicken, rice, and bell pepper to the pot and return to a boil. Decrease the heat to low and simmer for 25 minutes, or until all the liquid is absorbed. Remove from the heat and allow the mixture to cool.

2 multivitamins (One A Day Men's formula preferred)

2 (50 mg) zinc tablets

Crush the multivitamin and zinc tablets and add the powder to a food processor.

1 Brazil nut

¼ cup soy lecithin granules

2½ teaspoons Eggshell Powder (page 15)

2 teaspoons dried kelp powder

1 teaspoon potassium chloride

3 tablespoons canola oil

Add the Brazil nut, soy lecithin, Eggshell Powder, dried kelp powder, potassium chloride, and canola oil to the food processor and process until combined and the Brazil nuts have been reduced to the size of small meal.

2 cups low-fat cottage cheese

Combine the cottage cheese, chicken-rice mixture, and supplement mixture in a large bowl and stir well to evenly distribute the ingredients.

YIELD: 11 cups; 325 calories per cup

DAILY PORTION

Divide into two meals, or serve one-half the daily portion per day with one-half the normal amount of dry food.

10-POUND DOG	20-POUND DOG	40-POUND DOG	60-POUND DOG	80-POUND DOG
¾ to 1¼ cups	1½ to 2 cups	2⅓ to 3¼ cups	3⅓ to 4¼ cups	4¼ to 5¼ cups

WEIGHT LOSS

The key to losing weight, whether for man or beast, is to exercise more and eat less. Sounds easy, but it's difficult to put into practice. When Rover comes begging because his stomach is growling, it's hard to resist those puppy-dog eyes. And just because Rover is eating less doesn't mean his requirements for protein, vitamins, and minerals are reduced. The objective should be to provide foods that are low calorie, meaning less calories per cup of food, and still high in nutrition. The recipes for Turkey Minestrone (page 106) and Slow-Cooked Chicken and Barley (page 104) provide more bulk and fewer calories per cup. They also have a healthy serving of vegetables to help provide nutrients that your dog needs.

To reduce calories, determine your dog's current weight and use the chart here to determine calories per day. The goal for most dogs is to lose about 1 percent per week over a period of 4 to 12 weeks. If your dog needs to lose more than 2 to 5 pounds, aim at first for achieving the next lower weight. Once the target weight is reached, reduce calories again to meet the next goal. This will help your dog slowly lose weight without a sudden drop in the quantity of food, which will keep your pet satisfied and prevent you from feeling guilty.

Another method of reducing calories is to replace a portion of your dog's kibble with lower-calorie foods. Try replacing one-quarter of the kibble with an equal measure of potatoes or yams. His tummy will stay full and you'll reduce his caloric intake by 15 percent. Over the course of a week, that's like skipping a whole day's worth of meals. Don't add any butter or fat, because that adds calories right back in.

Aim to walk your dog for at least 40 minutes a day. If your dog is lethargic and more interested in the food bowl than a stroll around the block, start out slow with a couple of blocks and work your way up. We know ourselves that losing weight takes both patience and perseverance.

Weigh your dog regularly when on a weight-loss program or even when changing feeding regimens. When your dog reaches the ideal weight, congratulations! Now it's time to go back to the calories you'd feed at that ideal weight and activity level.

Dogs are a lot like us, though, in that not everybody fits the standard. If you're already feeding your dog below the recommended calories and your dog still isn't losing a few pounds, make an appointment with your veterinarian to determine what will work best. It's better to seek your veterinarian's assistance right away in order to keep your dog's lines in line than to need extra care later because of weight-related diseases.

Below are daily feeding sizes for two of the most filling recipes that are also lower in calories.

		DAILY PORTION	
CURRENT WEIGHT IN POUNDS	DAILY CALORIES TO ACHIEVE WEIGHT LOSS	SLOW-COOKED CHICKEN AND BARLEY	LAZYSAGNE
4	120	½ cup	½ cup
5	140	½ cup	⅔ cup
8	180	⅔ cup	¾ cup
10	210	¾ cup	1 cup
12	230	1 cup	1 cup
15	270	1 cup	1 cup
18	320	1¼ cups	1⅓ cups
20	340	1⅓ cups	1½ cups
25	410	1½ cups	1¾ cups
30	480	1¾ cups	2 cups
35	550	2 cups	2⅓ cups
40	620	2⅓ cups	2⅔ cups
45	680	2⅔ cups	3 cups
50	750	2¾ cups	3¼ cups
55	820	3 cups	3½ cups
60	890	3½ cups	3⅔ cups
65	960	3⅔ cups	4 cups
70	1,020	4 cups	4½ cups
75	1,090	4¼ cups	4⅔ cups
80	1,160	4½ cups	5 cups
85	1,230	4⅔ cups	5⅓ cups
90	1,300	5 cups	5⅔ cups
95	1,370	5¼ cups	6 cups
100	1,430	5½ cups	6¼ cups
105	1,500	5¾ cups	6½ cups
110	1,570	6 cups	6¾ cups
115	1,640	6⅓ cups	7 cups
120	1,710	6½ cups	7⅓ cups
125	1,770	6¾ cups	7⅔ cups
130	1,840	7 cups	8 cups

Continued

		DAILY PORTION	
CURRENT WEIGHT IN POUNDS	**DAILY CALORIES TO ACHIEVE WEIGHT LOSS**	**SLOW-COOKED CHICKEN AND BARLEY**	**LAZYSAGNE**
140	1,980	7⅔ cups	8⅔ cups
145	2,050	7¾ cups	9 cups
150	2,120	8 cups	9¼ cups
155	2,180	8⅓ cups	9½ cups
160	2,250	8⅔ cups	9¾ cups
170	2,390	9 cups	10⅓ cups
180	2,520	9⅔ cups	11 cups
190	2,660	10¼ cups	11½ cups
200	2,800	10¾ cups	12 cups

Slow Cooked Chicken and Barley has 260 calories per cup; Lazysagne has 230 calories per cup.

CANINE CALCULATION: WHEN VIOLET NEEDS TO SHRINK

Violet is a pretty hefty gal, tipping the scale at 85 pounds rather than the slender 70 pounds her frame was intended to support. Fear not, Violet; by taking you down in steps, we can help you reach your target weight and slowly decrease calories without leaving you hungry.

CURRENT WEIGHT	TARGET WEIGHT	TIME TO REACH TARGET WEIGHT	CALORIES TO REACH TARGET WEIGHT
85 lbs.	80 lbs.	Weeks 1-12	1,230
80 lbs.	75 lbs.	Weeks 13-24	1,160
75 lbs.	70 lbs.	Weeks 25-36	1,090
70 lbs.		Weeks 37+	1,270*

* Violet is returned to the calories for an inactive 70-pound dog as long as she maintains her weight.

The recipe for Slow-Cooked Chicken and Barley on page 104 is formulated for dogs like Violet, as is the method of slowly dropping calories illustrated here.

CHOOSING A COMMERCIAL DRY DOG FOOD

Dry food is the most popular type of pet food in the United States for its convenience, economy, and reliability to provide your dog with 100 percent of the necessary nutrients.

Itching is probably the number-one complaint from people about dogs and their food, and the finger of blame is usually pointed toward an undiagnosed food allergy. When I ask people what food they feed, I often want to cringe, because they're feeding a bargain food with more grains in it than meat. Commercial foods that rely heavily on grains are "complete and balanced" as far as scientists are concerned; but if your dog fails to thrive on them, the food is not doing its job. It's not always a true allergic reaction; sometimes it's just poor-quality food. On the other side, people often go overboard by saying that dogs shouldn't have any grains. There is a middle ground. What if we just didn't select foods that were predominately grains, especially corn?

One of my Dog Stew customers has a beautiful Lab named Paddy, who was breaking out in hot spots and itching like crazy. Paddy was being fed a pretty good commercial dry food that I once had Jackson eating. When we transitioned Paddy to fresh food, he was eating all three of my basic recipes, which included rice, barley, or oatmeal. When his owners called me after one week of Paddy's being on the food, they were extremely excited about his improvement. I didn't believe the change could happen so quickly, so when I delivered the food the following week, I inspected him for myself. His hot spots were improving and the incessant itching had stopped. It wasn't just having grain in his food that was causing problems; it was the quality and quantity of the grains. As my clientele expanded, I had opportunities to feed other dogs who were on the same exact dry food with the same conditions. I still fed them grains, and their skin problems all cleared up.

If you have a concern about allergies, ask your veterinarian to recommend a specialist. But also look carefully at the food you are feeding and question whether it measures up.

Dogs often develop skin conditions and become bored with their dry food. Although the common mantra is feed one food for life, it makes more sense to try rotating through different foods to provide variety and simply avoid digestive upset by gradually introducing new dry foods. This will also prevent dogs from developing allergies from being fed one food for life, as often happens.

IN THE PET FOOD AISLE

When shopping for commercial dog food, take a few minutes to review the ingredients panel. The first half of the label should list quality foods that you can readily identify, because these will make up the bulk of your dog's diet. Often when particular ingredients are listed it's by scientific names, so definitely ask the staff at your local pet store to help you understand the ingredients panel. If the staff doesn't know, then they should be able to easily look it up. If they can't look it up, try another pet store.

The following chart breaks down the quality of common ingredients; within each box, items are ranked by desirability, with the more preferable ingredients at the top of the list.

	POOR QUALITY: LEAVE IT ON THE SHELF	OK WITH HIGHER-QUALITY INGREDIENTS	BETTER QUALITY: PUT IT IN THE BOWL

MEAT	Poultry Digest
	Animal Digest
	Meat By-Products
	Meat and Bonemeal
	By-Product Meals
	Blood Meal
		Dried Egg Product
		Salmon Meal
		Fish Meal
		Cheese Product
		Hydrolyzed Soy Protein Isolate
			Eggs
			Named Meats: Chicken,
			  Beef, Lamb, Turkey, Duck,
			  Salmon, etc.
			Liver, Heart, Kidneys—when
			  specified by specific type of
			  animal source

VEGETABLES, FRUIT	Beet Pulp
	Potato Product or Potato
	  Starch
	Peanut Hulls
	Soybean Mill Run
	Powdered Cellulose
	Grape Pomace
	Citrus Pulp
		Tomato Pomace
		Apple Pomace
		Potatoes
		Celery
		Pea Starch or Pea Fiber
			Yams, Sweet Potatoes,
			  Pumpkin
			Leafy Green Vegetables:
			  Spinach, Kale, Parsley
			Peas, Carrots, Green Beans,
			  Broccoli, Zucchini
			Apples, Bananas, Other Fruits
			Cranberries, Blueberries

GRAINS	Flours (Wheat, Barley, etc.)
	Brewer's Rice, Rice Gluten
	Soy, Soy Flour, Soybeans,
	  Soy Grits
	Sorghum, Milo
	Cornstarch, Corn Gluten Meal
	Wheat Mill Run
		White Rice
		Whole-Grain Wheat
		Ground Whole Corn
		The same grain split into
		  separate ingredients
		Rice Bran
		Alfalfa Meal
			Amaranth, Millet, Oat Groats,
			  Quinoa
			Oats
			Barley, Rye
			Brown Rice
			Tapioca

FATS	Animal Fat Beef Tallow Mineral Oil Soybean Oil Cottonseed Oil	Vegetable Oil Canola Oil Safflower Oil	Salmon Oil Fish Oil Chicken Fat Flax Oil Olive Oil Safflower Oil

PRESERVATIVES	BHA (Butylated
	  Hydroxysanisole)
	BHT (Butylated
	  Hydroxytoluene)
	Ethoxyquin
	TBHQ (Tertiary
	  Butylhydroquinone)
	Sodium Metabisulphite
		Citric Acid	Rosemary Extract
			Other Herbs and Extracts
			Vitamin E (Mixed Tocopherols)

VITAMINS MINERALS	Menadione or Vitamin K
	  supplement
	Zinc Oxide
	Iron Oxide
		Non-Chelated Minerals
		Hydroxyapatite (Calcium)
		Psyllium Seed Husks
			Chelated or Sequestered Min-
			  erals
			Flaxseed
			Lactobacillus acidophilus
			Yucca schidigera

ADDITIVES	Sugar "Meat Broth" High-Fructose Corn Syrup Food Colorings/Dyes	Salt Molasses Liver Flavor	Chicken Broth, Beef Broth, etc. Apple Cider Vinegar

How to Read a Label

Ingredients are listed according to their predominance by weight; the higher the item is on the ingredients panel, the more your dog is depending on it to provide nutrition. Just like you, nutrition for your dog is best sourced from whole foods rather than by depending solely on vitamins thrown in at the end. Don't be surprised that there are so many vitamins and minerals added; manufacturers want to cover all the bases.

Two examples:

(The size of the type has been altered to illustrate approximate proportions.)

The first example is the food that I use to supplement the home-cooked meals for my own dogs.

Meat is the first ingredient, so we're off to a good start. Chicken meal is next, and then shortly after that come turkey and fish meals—that's a good amount of meat. The only caution about this food comes in early; three sources of protein may aggravate dogs with allergies. Dogs with allergies should stick to a single source of protein. For dogs without allergic conditions, this food supplies more diverse proteins and can be a healthy choice.

Oatmeal is pretty far down the list, with flaxseed and a smidge of barley (way down on the list) being the only other grains included, so grains make up a small amount of this food. Carrots, sweet potatoes (whole, not just the skins), blueberries, and cranberries are all great additions to your dog's meal.

Notice that salt appears way down on the list of ingredients. The manufacturer has added so many good ingredients they don't need to pump the flavor up with salt.

There are no preservatives that raise flags here. This manufacturer is obviously proud of their ingredients, and they should be. If you can find a food like this, you can feel comfortable putting it in the bowl.

When reading the fine print, you'll notice the manufacturer includes some interesting ingredients:

- Glucosamine is added for joint health.
- *Yucca schidigera* extract helps to reduce stool odors and excessive gas.
- Green tea extract contains antioxidants and is believed to help protect against cancer.
- Dried chicory root is used as a source of fiber rather than low-quality products like peanut shell hulls or beet pulp.

Foods like this are best found at local and independent specialty pet stores. My experience has been that the smaller the store, the more knowledgeable the staff and the better the quality of the foods sold.

THE MAIN COURSE

First two
to three
ingredients

THE SIDE DISHES

Fourth ingredient
to first added fat

THE GARNISH

First ingredient after
fat to first vitamin

EVERYTHING THAT COULDN'T BE PROVIDED BY THE ABOVE

Vitamins, minerals, and
preservatives

Deboned chicken, chicken meal,

potato starch, turkey meal, fish meal, tomato pomace, chicken fat,*

natural chicken flavor, oatmeal,
whole carrots, whole sweet potatoes,
blueberries, cranberries, flaxseed,
grass, dried parsley, alfalfa meal, kelp meal,

taurine, L-carnitine, L-lysine, glucosamine hydrochloride,
Yucca schidigera extract, green tea extract, turmeric, herring
oil, fructooligosaccharides, monooligosaccharides, dried
chicory root, black malted barley, oil of rosemary, vitamin
A supplement, vitamin C, vitamin E supplement,
vitamin D_3 supplement, beta carotene, calcium
ascorbate, vitamin B_{12} supplement, niacin, calcium
pantothenate, riboflavin, pyridoxine hydrochloride,
thiamine hydrochloride, folic acid, biotin,
choline chloride, calcium chloride, zinc amino
acid complex, iron amino acid complex,
copper amino acid complex, manganese
amino acid complex, potassium amino
acid complex, cobalt proteinate,
potassium chloride, sodium
selenite, salt, Lactobacillus
acidophilus, Bacillus
subtilis, Bifidobacterium
thermophilum,
Bifidobacterium
longum, Enterococcus
faecium.
*preserved with
natural mixed
tocopherols

This second example doesn't fare as well, and it wouldn't be surprising if your dog didn't do so well on this food.

THE MAIN COURSE

Really? Corn as the main ingredient? And by-products?

THE SIDE DISHES

Grains far outweigh meat—not good.

THE GARNISH

Beef is added as the garnish, not a main ingredient—along with sugar, which your dog doesn't need.

VITAMINS AND PRESERVATIVES

There is more salt in this than dried peas and carrots. Lower-quality ingredients require the addition of a lot of vitamins, minerals, and amino acids.

Ground yellow corn,
chicken by-product meal,

corn gluten meal,
whole-wheat flour,
animal fat,*

rice flour, beef, soy flour,
sugar, sorbitol,

tricalcium phosphate, water, salt, phosphoric acid, animal digest, potassium chloride, dicalcium phosphate, sorbic acid (a preservative), L-lysine monohydrochloride, dried peas, dried carrots, calcium carbonate, calcium propionate (a preservative), choline chloride, added color (Yellow 5, Red 40, Yellow 6, Blue 2), DL-methionine, vitamin E supplement, zinc sulfate, ferrous sulfate, vitamin A supplement, manganese sulfate, niacin, vitamin B_{12} supplement, calcium pantothenate, riboflavin supplement, copper sulfate, biotin, garlic oil, thiamine hydrochloride, pyridoxine hydrochloride, thiamine mononitrate, folic acid, vitamin D_3 supplement, menadione sodium bisulfite complex (source of vitamin K activity), calcium iodate, sodium selenite. *preserved with mixed tocopherols (form of vitamin E)

Corn is the first and third ingredient, leaving your dog depending on a grain for the majority of nutrition. Corn does provide some necessary nutrients, but it's a lot of bulk without a lot of punch. Corn is valued for its high linoleic (omega-6) acid content in comparison with other grains, but ¼ teaspoon of flaxseed oil contains almost as much omega-6 fatty acids as a cup of ground corn and a better proportion of omega-3 oils. In the United States, corn is quite inexpensive, so it's easy on the manufacturer's budget, but it's far from a high-quality ingredient.

By the AAFCO (American Association of Feed Control Officials) definition, chicken by-product meal consists of necks, feet, undeveloped eggs, and intestines. Although some nutrients do exist in these animal parts, are they really the best nourishment for your best friend? If the ingredients panel contains the word *by-product*, say "bye-bye."

Animal fat comes in the middle, but from what kind of animal? Generic terms mean that the manufacturer isn't held to using one particular source, and so it can contain any type of animal. If you consistently feed your dog the same brand of food and all of a sudden your dog is not doing well on the food, it may be that the source of generic items like this has been changed.

The manufacturer advertises this food as: "Moist, chewy chunks made with real beef are rich in quality protein to help build strong muscles." But there's really not much beef inside, given that the beef is sandwiched between animal fat and sugar.

Your dog has no nutritional requirement for sugar and sorbitol. These taste-enhancing ingredients are still included because dogs do have an affinity for sweet flavors, and without them the food probably wouldn't interest your dog as much.

By definition animal digest, which appears in a small amount, cannot contain hair, horns, teeth, hooves, or feathers. That's a comfort. The bad news is that it's very generic, so you have no idea what kind of animal or parts are used, and the composition may change from batch to batch.

The manufacturer includes dried peas and carrots, which sound great on the label, but there's more salt in this food than there are peas or carrots. It's unfortunate that peas and carrots are featured predominately on this food's packaging but not inside the bag.

Then the manufacturer adds red, yellow, and blue food colorings. Your dog doesn't care what color the food is, so why should these be necessary? On the plus side, there are no preservatives in this food to raise concerns.

CANINE CALCULATION: SPEND A LITTLE, SAVE A LOT

A note on cost: The first example was a 30-pound bag available for $38. The second example was a 31-pound bag available for $27. As with most things, you'll get what you pay for. With nutrition being the key component of good health, it might benefit you to hedge your bets on paying a little extra every month for a better-quality food.

$38.00 - $27.00 = $11.00 added cost

$11.00 x 12 months = $132.00/year

$132.00 x 14 years = $1,848/lifetime additional food costs

In comparison, my veterinarian bills for Jackson's lymphoma alone were more than $7,000. Baxter's diabetes treatment with insulin, blood tests, and office visits total about $1,500 per year, as does medication and treatment for Chloe's heart disease.

This food and others like it are very well marketed. I see ads in magazines and television commercials all the time for this very food. If the food is so inexpensive at retail and the manufacturer is spending so much money on advertising, it's understandable that they don't have much left over for high-quality ingredients. The more advertising I see for a brand, the less likely I am to buy it.

TRANSITIONING FOODS

When transitioning from one commercial food to another, always do so gradually. The following chart illustrates the proportion of new and old foods over the course of a week. If your dog has a sensitive stomach, you can perform the same transition over two to three weeks to avoid upset.

	CURRENT FOOD	NEW FOOD
DAY 1	75%	25%
DAY 2	75%	25%
DAY 3	50%	50%
DAY 4	50%	50%
DAY 5	25%	75%
DAY 6	25%	75%
DAY 7	0%	100%

Your best friend rolls over.

A MORE MEANINGFUL MEALTIME

Feeding isn't just about what you feed your dog;
it's also about how you feed your best friend.

When we provide food to our dogs, whether it is a treat or a meal, it's an important act that deserves more respect from our dogs and ourselves. Too often we rush through the process; we scoop food into the bowl, and then get trampled by our dogs as we set the bowl in place. For our dogs it's a race; for us it's a chore. You're going to feed your dog more than 700 times this year alone. Why not slow it down just a bit and create a calmer, more meaningful, and more enjoyable routine?

SETTING THE TABLE AT FLOOR LEVEL

Before you put anything in the bowl, there are a few things you might want to consider when selecting and maintaining the dishes you use to feed your best friend and setting up his food station.

- Water and food bowls should be stainless steel or lead-free ceramic. American ceramics are mostly free of lead, but foreign-made ceramics may contain high levels of lead, which may leach into water. Avoid plastics and aluminum because they also may leach chemicals, and glass bowls, which may break more easily than ceramic dishes.
- Inspect dishes often for chips or cracks and replace as necessary. If a dish suddenly breaks while your dog is eating, it's doubtful your dog would pause.
- Consider a raised feeding station that doesn't require your dog's head to dip below shoulder level when eating. This is especially helpful with senior pets.
- *A bowl licked clean is not a clean bowl.* Provide a clean bowl at each meal to eliminate the opportunity for bacteria to build up. Sometimes dogs who are sick or have diarrhea just need to have their bowl cleaned more consistently. We've started using cereal and pasta bowls because they fit easily into our dishwasher. You can get a nice set to use in rotation at thrift stores or garage sales.

RINGING THE DINNER BELL

Creating a more meaningful mealtime starts with the way you give your best friend his food. You'll find information on specific problem mealtime behaviors later in this chapter, but first a few tips for increasing both your pet's and your own enjoyment of mealtime:

- When it's time for a meal, call your dog into the feeding area and tell your dog to sit and stay.
- While your dog remains in place, dish out the proper serving, keeping one eye on your pet.
- If you're serving a homemade meal, which may have congealed upon cooling, warm it up just a bit or add warm water. Meals served at just a few degrees above room temperature will release

a little aroma that adds to the experience for your dog. Adding water will also help with digestion and absorption of the nutrients.

- While your dog still remains in place, slowly set the bowl down. If your dog suddenly makes a lunge for the bowl, stand back up with the bowl in your hand. Every time your dog moves in a forward motion without permission, you should move in reverse to your original standing position. Move slower and slower in your successive attempts to put the bowl on the ground while your dog remains in place. Please don't be frustrated if it takes a few attempts. If this is a new behavior, your dog may not understand why there is a sudden shift in the routine.

- If at any time your dog moves or attempts to follow you, freeze in place. If your dog does not move back to the starting position without prompting, set the dog bowl on a countertop, lead your dog back to the starting place, and start all over.

- When the bowl finally makes it to the floor, stand in place and take a deep breath. Relax. Then calmly give the word for your dog to go eat. At our house we say, "Mangia!" as a special phrase reserved for mealtime.

Developing a new mealtime routine takes practice, but your dog can learn to wait patiently if you have the patience to follow through with the routine. It can take a few weeks, but you are not developing a new routine for just tonight or even next week. When you take the time to create a more rewarding routine, you're developing a stronger bond with your dog for the 7,000-plus meals over your dog's lifetime.

Free feeding dry food is not recommended. Your dog will not starve while you're at work all day, and you can always leave a stuffed Kong as a snack. Fresh foods should not be left out for any longer than 30 minutes to prevent the buildup of bacteria.

Water

With two-thirds of your dog's weight composed of water, this is one of the most important components of your dog's diet. Water aids in digestion and the absorption of nutrients and is essential for helping your pet maintain body temperature.

- As a general rule, provide at least 2½ times as much water per day as the amount of food your dog eats. Especially in hot weather, it's important that your dog has access to an abundance of fresh, clean water.

- When preparing a meal, pick up and clean both water and food bowls and provide fresh water. Consider pouring unused water on houseplants or on the garden to conserve resources.

- Tap water should be run for a minute before filling the bowl to clear the buildup of minerals or toxins in the pipes.

- If you use bottled water for yourself or in your own cooking, consider giving your best friend the same. If you don't like the taste of your tap water, your best friend might not either.

- If your dog's water consumption changes dramatically by either increasing or decreasing, consult your vet.
- Fresh food contains a lot of moisture, so that will help meet part of your dog's requirement, but still make sure to have more than enough water available.
- If you feed mostly dry food, consider adding 1 part water to every 2 parts dry food to help meet your dog's requirement for water.
- Dogs who spend a great deal of times outdoors in summer or winter will need additional water.
- When you take your dog hiking or camping, bring additional water for your dog to drink. Do not let your dog drink from standing water or water with algae growing in it. If possible, try to prevent your dog from drinking from streams, as the water may contain dangerous bacteria or protozoa. (In September 2009, four dogs died in separate incidents when they drank from Elk Creek in Oregon.)

PROBLEM MEALTIME BEHAVIORS

It's unfortunate that the table manners of our canine companions have not evolved as much as our relationships with them have. When we cannot predict a dog's behavior around food, it can become worrisome, or it can become annoying when it's as predictable as a 5 a.m. alarm. Modifying problem behaviors will require consistency, trust, and in many cases a new set of rules. In most cases, a few weeks of repeating a pattern will clue your dog into the new paradigm and be well worth the effort since the results will be repeated for thousands more meals.

However, good luck on getting your dog to chew with his mouth closed.

Begging

A common misconception is that feeding your dog anything but commercial dog food or treats will encourage your dog to beg. Food doesn't encourage your dog to beg—the routines you set with your dog do. If you feed your dog at the table, your dog will learn to hang out around the table waiting for his share. If you feed your dog in the kitchen, your dog will learn the kitchen is a great place to score some extra vittles. There's no question about it: Dogs like to eat and will repeat behaviors that have enabled them to acquire food.

Teach your dog to wait outside of the dining room with the following routine.

- When you sit down with your dinner, bring a treat to the table for the dog. (Don't advertise that you have the treat.)
- After setting your meal on the table, lead the dog outside of the room and tell your dog to sit and stay.

Your best friend has a tough exterior.

- 🐾 Provide one small treat, repeat the stay command, and enjoy your meal.
- 🐾 Firmly say "No" if your dog begins to move, and if necessary lead your dog back to the exact position again, but this time without a treat.
- 🐾 When you are done with your meal, walk over to your dog, treat in hand. Do not call your dog over to you, as this reinforces that treats are fed in the dining room.
- 🐾 Praise your dog repeatedly with "Good dog, good stay."
- 🐾 Hand over the treat and praise again.
- 🐾 Release your dog from the stay position. We use, "Okay, go!"
- 🐾 If your dog immediately goes to the dining room, firmly say "No," and lead your dog away.

The deal is that your dog has to stay in place until you have fed the treat and released the dog from the stay position—otherwise no payoff. It takes a while to learn, but remember that your dog will repeat behaviors that have worked in the past. With repetition, your dog can learn this improved behavior.

Counter Surfing/Breaking and Entering

When I adopted Jackson, he had already learned to open a cupboard by himself, so he threw his own garbage parties, which entertains the dog but frustrates the cleanup crew. We later started keeping a lock on the garbage cupboard, but if we ever left it open Jackson remembered how to get what he wanted.

Jackson had stolen steaks, bread, crackers, and cheese off of the countertop when left unattended for even just a few moments. His counter surfing was one of the most difficult behaviors I've had to stop. I tried double-sided tape on the countertops, and for some dogs tape sticking to their paws is enough to scare them away for life, but not Jackson. He tore off the tape and ran through the house with it, then tore the tape into little tiny bits.

One day Jackson stole a blueberry pie and was hopped up on sugar for the entire evening. He was spinning in circles, barking and running up and down the hallway trying to relieve his sugar high. Frustrated, I knew I had to put a stop to his raids once and for all, so I asked myself, "What am I doing wrong that allows this to happen?" Up until that point, it was always about Jackson's behavior and blaming him, but then it occurred to me that it's my responsibility to keep the counters clear and prevent Jackson from getting his paws on my pie. Since then I've turned the car around numerous times when I thought something might be left on the counter. It's always better to be safe than sorry.

Here are a few more tips to discourage counter raids:

- 🐾 If you're sharing (approved) scraps from your meal preparation, put them in your dog's bowl or feed in a room outside of the kitchen. Avoid feeding your dog directly as you prepare food on the counter.

- If your dog is underfoot while you are preparing food, it's dangerous to both of you. I've almost tripped over a dog more than once while carrying a hot pan. Tell your dog "Out of the kitchen" anytime that food is out or meals are being prepared.

- Keep counters clear at all times, even if you are just going out to light the barbecue; it's an opportunity for steaks to be stolen. If your dog performs a regular check of the countertops, prevent possible injuries by clearing the counters of glass or other breakables.

- Unless you discover a robbery in progress, you can't really punish your dog, because your dog will likely not connect his original action and your reaction. However, you can be upset, just not at the dog. It's okay to say, "Where's my pie?" in a stern voice while pointing at the empty pie pan. Just don't direct your anger at your dog. As strange as it may seem, vent your frustration on the pie pan. Your dog may sulk and act guilty, but it doesn't necessarily mean the dog is personally taking responsibility; he just doesn't want to be associated with a "bad" pie pan.

- If you have concerns about the foods or quantity consumed, or if your pet begins to act lethargic, has excessive diarrhea or constipation, or begins to vomit, seek help immediately. You can contact your veterinarian or the ASPCA's poison control center at (888) 426-4435.

Early Morning Wake-Up Calls

There's nothing worse than trying to sleep and having your dog wake you up for breakfast. It's understandable when a dog wakes you up to go to the bathroom, but when it's simply because you're the chef and she's ready to place her order, the system is broken. Here are a few things to try:

- Feed your dog regular meals twice a day to prevent the extremes of hunger and fullness.

- Ensure your dog is getting enough exercise by adding an additional walk in the evening before bed.

- Don't feed your dog the first thing after you get up. Sometimes feed your dog before your shower, sometimes after. Get up, get the paper, make some coffee, and leave the kitchen for a few minutes. Then eventually, casually even, ask your dog to follow you back to the kitchen with a simple, "Come."

- Don't make a big deal out of breakfast time by asking your dog, "Are you ready for breakfast?" or "Are you hungry?" You probably already know the answer, so there's no reason to get her excited.

- Make your dog sit patiently while you are preparing her meal. If she moves, freeze! Don't continue until your dog is sitting and waiting calmly. Drooling, however, is reluctantly acceptable.

- If it's really bad and your dog isn't learning, step up the methodology. Fill an empty soda can with some pennies and put it by your bed. When your dog sounds the wake-up call, shake the can loudly, say "No," and try to go back to sleep.

- Under no circumstances should you immediately get up and feed your dog.

- 🐾 Lead your dog from the room if necessary or let her out to relieve herself. Put as much time between when you get up and when you feed your dog as possible. Go back to bed and wait it out for at least 20 minutes, or better yet, try to fall asleep.
- 🐾 If the pennies don't work, try a whistle.
- 🐾 If the whistle doesn't work, try banging on a pot with a spoon.

Your dog may not get it overnight, but you're awake anyway, so you might as well invest in some training so you can sleep in next week.

Aggression/Food Guarding

It's pretty scary to have a dog turn on you, especially when it's your own. Instinctively, your dog wants to enjoy a meal without the fear of it being taken away, so it's important to establish trust. This regimen will slowly acclimatize your dog to sharing space with you and his food bowl:

- 🐾 Dish your dog's food into the bowl, but then find a comfortable place to sit, with the bowl in your lap.
- 🐾 Call your dog and tell your dog to sit facing you.
- 🐾 When your dog is sitting calmly, scoop about one-eighth of the food into the palm of your hand.
- 🐾 Allow your dog to eat the first handful. When the first scoop is gone, pause for about five seconds before scooping some more and repeating the feeding process until the meal is gone. Count out the five seconds in your head, not aloud. Five seconds is a long enough interval to teach patience without being so long that it will create anxiety.
- 🐾 When the meal is finished, raise your hands with your palms facing your dog and say, "All gone." Then set the bowl down and let your dog inspect it so that he can ensure it really is all gone.
- 🐾 In the second week, measure out your dog's food in a separate bowl and slowly fill portions into a food bowl on the floor between you.
- 🐾 When your dog is responding well, return the empty food bowl to its regular place. Your dog should always sit and stay while you are preparing food and not approach the bowl until you give your permission. Drop in a portion at a time while you are standing nearby.
- 🐾 On an ongoing basis, drop in extra (approved) tidbits or a bit of the reserved meal portion. This is also something that should be done with puppies from the very beginning to prevent food guarding later.

Establishing trust takes time, so be patient with this process. Although it takes a few extra minutes now, you're establishing a bond that will last for the life of your dog. Yes, it's a messy process, but that's why there's soap.

Under no circumstances should you place yourself in danger. If your dog growls or you fear that your dog may bite, contact a qualified trainer.

Speed Eating

Few dogs eat at a leisurely pace, but there are those that eat so fast they are literally gulping their food down. When dogs eat too quickly, they run the risk of choking or bloat because of the large amount of air that is ingested with the food. Bloat, also known as torsion, causes gas to be trapped in the dog's stomach when too much gas accumulates. This can be life-threatening, and when it happens once, it's more likely to happen again, with each repetition becoming more serious. Deep-chested dogs are particularly prone to bloat. Contact your veterinarian if your dog is a speed eater and begins to show any of the common signs of bloat: retching without vomiting successfully, excessive drooling, a firm abdomen, uncharacteristic discomfort in a standing or lying position, or sudden weakness.

Some dogs can be taught to eat more slowly; some have to be monitored at every meal. Try the same feeding program as suggested with aggressive eaters. If that doesn't work, it's time to go to extremes with one of these methods:

- Heat your dog's food to a temperature a little lower than that at which you would serve your own food.
- Freeze your dog's food and set your dog out in the yard to slowly eat the food while it thaws. The food doesn't necessarily have to be frozen all the way through, but it should be cold.
- Stuff the dog's food in a Kong or other puzzle toy, so that he has to work to get the food out.
- Feed your dog's meal in a Bundt cake pan, especially the type with lots of nooks and crannies.
- Spread your dog's food out onto a rimmed baking sheet.
- Invest in a food bowl specifically designed to slow down eating.
- Feed smaller meals more frequently.
- Put a clean rubber ball or two in your dog's dish so that he has to work around the ball to get the food. The balls should be large enough that your dog doesn't swallow them. Large, smooth stones work well too.

If you notice that a method is not working, finish the meal by hand feeding and then try a new method at the next mealtime.

Wait for an hour after mealtime before taking your speed eater for a walk or any extended activity.

Reluctant Eaters

It's not unusual for a dog to occasionally skip a meal, and for most a meal or two skipped per week is not a cause for alarm. If your dog refuses to eat for more than a day, you should first consult your veterinarian. Various diseases or dental problems could be causing your dog to prefer hunger over discomfort.

If everything checks out with the veterinarian, the next place to look is the food you are feeding. Although commercial foods are sold as "dog food," dogs really aren't interested that much in them if they contain less-desirable ingredients. Your dog's sense of smell is at least 100,000 times more acute than your own. If there are chemicals that smell iffy to your dog or your dog doesn't smell anything enticing, your dog may just pass it by. If your dog is holding out for something "better," then maybe you should provide something better. Who's to say that we make all the right decisions based on colorful packaging and promises made by pet food manufacturers?

It might be time to try a new food. See page 169 for guidelines on choosing a dry food. The quality of food can mean a big difference in your dog's health, so be prepared to spend a little more. As you introduce a new food, do it slowly.

If you're concerned about your pet eating, you probably also want your dog to enjoy mealtime as well. If your dog is crying out for something more interesting, bring some interest to the bowl with foods that are good additions to your pet's diet: some water, an egg, homemade stock, a spoonful of yogurt or pumpkin. Try spreading an irresistible cheese taste over your dog's food with a few swipes of Parmesan over a Microplane grater.

A few other hints might make mealtime more appealing:

- Ensure that your dog is not eating something elsewhere. Is the garbage can lid closed? Is the cat box mysteriously clean? Take extra precautions in these areas if necessary.
- Look at your dog's bowl and its location. Is your dog's bowl too deep, or too large? Does her collar make noise when it hits the bowl? Is your dog eating in a part of the house that feels comfortable? Something as simple as changing the bowl size, slipping off the dog collar before feeding, or ensuring your dog is not looking into a corner and is standing on a non-slippery surface can greatly ease your pet's fears around eating.
- Feed your dog twice a day, at the same hours each day. Senior dogs may want to eat less at each meal, so three meals a day could be helpful.
- Ensure that your pet is getting enough exercise; work up an appetite with a quick walk before each meal.

You and your best friend are the lifeblood of the community.

Contact your local Red Cross for opportunities for you to give blood,
and your local pet hospital for opportunities for your dog to help save a life.

ACKNOWLEDGMENTS

Although this book is a culmination of five years of research, recipe testing, and writing, I can hardly say that I did it alone. The support of family, friends, co-workers, collaborators, and pup-parents kept me motivated and helped to focus the voice of my words.

SALTY

You've brought not only dogs but also love into my life, and your support means the world to me. Thank you for listening to my endless ideas and providing your own while ensuring that we still make time to enjoy life. I sure do.

ALICIA DICKERSON GRIFFITH

A picture is worth a thousand words, and your contribution to this book has been a beautiful and realistic essay on the relationship between people and their dogs. Your vision has resulted in great visuals.

MICHELLE BRENES

I probably would never have ventured down this path without your suggestion: "You like dogs, you like to cook, so cook for dogs." Thanks for helping me realize what has become my life's work.

DOG STEW CUSTOMERS

You are great people who not only cherish your dogs but who also trusted me to help care for them. I appreciate your faith, suggestions, and encouragement.

SALLY EKUS

From the first day you received my proposal, you've been my cheerleader, my guide, my confidant, and a good friend. Thank you helping me realize what lies between these covers.

ADIDAS FINANCE

My friends, who just happen to be co-workers, have allowed me to derail many a meeting talking about dogs and the book's progress. Thank you for your patience and invaluable feedback.

CAROL GARDNER

At my lowest point, when I felt disaster looming, you inspired me to keep pushing forward and find a new avenue for success. This book is a result of that conversation. It's obvious where Zelda gets her wisdom.

RALEIGH, BAXTER, CHLOE, AND DUNCAN

My taste testers, companions for long hours at the keyboard, and my kitchen support. Thank you for pulling me away to go for walks, and for your incredible patience and love.

JANE CRIST

Mom, thank you for the endless days spent in the kitchen with me both at Dog Stew and at home. Everyone should have a mother as supportive and dedicated as you.

This book is dedicated to Jackson, but also to you.

LANE BUTLER

I asked a million questions and you provided a million answers. Thank you for understanding my vision and working with the team at Andrews McMeel to make it even better.

TIM LISZT

Thank you for your friendship foremost, for helping me figure out Dog Stew's visual identity, and for solving every Mac dilemma I encountered.

SUZANNE MARTIN

Many people have said, "I love your book." You were the first to say, "You can do better." I hope that I have and I appreciate your input.

KARLA THOMAS

I held this book so tightly to my chest for years. You were the first person to read it, and you showed me what worked and what needed to be reworked.

COLETTE PECK

I couldn't count the many hours you spent cleaning up the kitchen behind me and ensuring that I double-checked everything. Your attention to detail improved mine.

RYAN FICEK

Thank you for being such a great friend, "little brother," and guardian for our pack.

MAC AND WENDY SETTER

Thanks for giving me a place to write, a kitchen test in, dogs to feed, and a wonderful place to retreat.

RESOURCES

Web Sites for Supplements

- 🐾 NOW Foods: manufacturer of herbs and human vitamin supplements. www.nowfoods.com
- 🐾 Drs. Foster & Smith: everything under the sun for your pet, including vitamins. www.drsfostersmith.com
- 🐾 Grizzly Pet Products: offers high-quality salmon oil at retailers and online; I appreciate the technical information that they shared with me about their product. www.grizzlypetproducts.com

Information on Pet Foods

- 🐾 *Whole Dog Journal*: a great periodical for all dog nutrition, training, and pet care advice. I really appreciate their annual review of dog food brands for an objective opinion.
- 🐾 www.whole-dog-journal.com
- 🐾 Dog Food Advisor: a good source for analysis and rating of commercial dog foods. www.dogfoodadvisor.com
- 🐾 *Feed Your Pet Right*, by Marion Nestle and Malden C. Nesheim (Free Press, 2010), offers insight into the pet food industry and helps readers understand the complicated maze of pet food choices.
- 🐾 *K9 Kitchen*, by Monica Segal (Doggie Dinner, Inc., 2002), provides information on raw-food diets and a sensible opinion on the difference between raw foods and home-cooked meals.

Information on Canine Nutrition

Sources of information that I found invaluable in researching canine nutrition, these are more reliable and well researched than what can be retrieved by most Internet search engines:

- 🐾 *Nutrient Requirements of Cats and Dogs* from the National Research Council (National Academies Press, 2006).
- 🐾 *Home-Prepared Dog & Cat Diets: the Healthful Alternative*, by Donald R. Strombeck, DVM, PhD (Wiley-Blackwell, 1999), offers in-depth, slightly more technical information on home-cooked meals. This is a great source of information for understanding the needs of dogs with medical issues.
- 🐾 *Canine Nutrition: What Every Owner, Breeder, and Trainer Should Know*, by Lowell Ackerman, DVM (Alpine Publications, 1999), offers similar information, especially regarding sick dogs.
- 🐾 *Small Animal Clinical Nutrition, 4th Edition (Mark Morris Associates, 2006)*, is extremely technical but has an incredible amount of detail.

- *The Inflammation-Free Diet Plan*, by Monica Reinagel *(McGraw-Hill, 2007)*, details how inflammation is caused and how choosing the right foods can help reduce inflammation.
- *101 Foods That Can Save Your Life*, by David Grotto, RD, LDN (Bantam, 2010), provides detailed information on the compounds in foods that prevent disease along with plenty of tasty recipes for your family.
- *Your Dog: The Owner's Manual*, by Dr. Mary Becker and Gina Spadafori (Grand Central Life & Style, 2011), contains lots of hints and information that you will find invaluable.
- Banfield Pet Hospitals provided information from their *State of Pet Health 2011* report, for which I am very grateful.

METRIC CONVERSIONS AND EQUIVALENTS

Approximate Metric Equivalents

VOLUME

¼ teaspoon	1 milliliter
½ teaspoon	2.5 milliliters
¾ teaspoon	4 milliliters
1 teaspoon	5 milliliters
1¼ teaspoons	6 milliliters
1½ teaspoons	7.5 milliliters
1¾ teaspoons	8.5 milliliters
2 teaspoons	10 milliliters
1 tablespoon (½ fluid ounce)	15 milliliters
2 tablespoons (1 fluid ounce)	30 milliliters
¼ cup	60 milliliters
⅓ cup	80 milliliters
½ cup (4 fluid ounces)	120 milliliters
⅔ cup	160 milliliters
¾ cup	180 milliliters
1 cup (8 fluid ounces)	240 milliliters
1¼ cups	300 milliliters
1½ cups (12 fluid ounces)	360 milliliters
1⅔ cups	400 milliliters
2 cups (1 pint)	460 milliliters
3 cups	700 milliliters
4 cups (1 quart)	.95 liter
1 quart plus ¼ cup	1 liter
4 quarts (1 gallon)	3.8 liters

WEIGHT

¼ ounce	7 grams
½ ounce	14 grams
¾ ounce	21 grams
1 ounce	28 grams
1¼ ounces	35 grams
1½ ounces	42.5 grams
1⅔ ounces	45 grams
2 ounces	57 grams
3 ounces	85 grams
4 ounces (¼ pound)	113 grams
5 ounces	142 grams
6 ounces	170 grams
7 ounces	198 grams
8 ounces (½ pound)	227 grams
16 ounces (1 pound)	454 grams
35.25 ounces (2.2 pounds)	1 kilogram

LENGTH

⅛ inch	3 millimeters
¼ inch	6 millimeters
½ inch	1¼ centimeters
1 inch	2½ centimeters
2 inches	5 centimeters
2½ inches	6 centimeters
4 inches	10 centimeters
5 inches	13 centimeters
6 inches	15¼ centimeters
10 inches	25½ centimeters
12 inches (1 foot)	30 centimeters

Metric Conversion Formulas

TO CONVERT	MULTIPLY
Ounces to grams	Ounces by 28.35
Pounds to kilograms	Pounds by .454
Teaspoons to milliliters	Teaspoons by 4.93
Tablespoons to milliliters	Tablespoons by 14.79
Cups to milliliters	Cups by 236.59
Cups to liters	Cups by .236
Inches to centimeters	Inches by 2.54

Oven Temperatures

To convert Fahrenheit to Celsius, subtract 32 from Fahrenheit, multiply the result by 5, then divide by 9.

DESCRIPTION	FAHRENHEIT	CELSIUS	BRITISH GAS MARK
Very cool	200°	95°	0
Very cool	225°	110°	¼
Very cool	250°	120°	½
Cool	275°	135°	1
Cool	300°	150°	2
Warm	325°	165°	3
Moderate	350°	175°	4
Moderately hot	375°	190°	5
Fairly hot	400°	200°	6
Hot	425°	220°	7
Very hot	450°	230°	8
Very hot	475°	245°	9

COMMON INGREDIENTS AND THEIR APPROXIMATE EQUIVALENTS

1 cup uncooked rice = 225 grams

1 cup panko bread crumbs = 60 grams

1 cup uncooked quick-cooking rolled oats = 156 grams

1 cup all-purpose flour = 140 grams

1 cup uncooked quinoa = 170 grams

1 cup dried cranberries = 120 grams

1 cup pearl barley = 200 grams

1 cup canned pumpkin = 245 grams (homemade versions can
     vary from this depending on water content)

1 cup grated cheddar cheese = 113 grams

3 teaspoons/1 tablespoon Eggshell Powder = 20 grams

10 ounces frozen green beans = 1¾ cups

1 cup chopped fresh parsley = 60 grams

1 cup uncooked chicken livers = 165 grams

Information compiled from the USDA's National Nutrient Database for Standard Reference.

Your best friend drinks it all in.

INDEX

omega-3 fatty acids *(continued)*
   as anti-inflammatory agent, 4
   as fats, 4
   kidney function, promoting, 158
omega-6 fatty acids
   causing inflammation, 4
   as fats, 4
   kidney function, promoting, 158
onions, 25
oranges, 30
overweight dogs, 19, 22, 154

P

pancakes
   Blueberry Pancakes, 42
   Dutch Baby Pancake, 40
papayas, 29
Parmesan
   Pup's Parmesan Cookies, 82
   Wonton, Meet Parmesan, 59
parsley, 31
   Puppy Pesto, 69
peanut butter, 34
   Cheerios and, as Kong stuffing, 49
   making your own, 79
   Peanut Butter and Banana Ice Cream, 58
   Peanut Butter and Cinnamon Cookies, 79
pears, 29
peas
   Cancer-Fighting Split-Pea Soup, 143
   Green Pea Christmas Trees, 83
   snap, 31
phenylalanine, 3
phosphorus, 6, 157
phytochemicals, xvi
pits, from fruit, 26
plums and apricots, 30
pork
   bacon, 34, 92
   Pork and Penne, 122
portion size
   for active dogs, 18
   calorie recommendations and, 19–21, 166
   for extra-active dogs, 18
   for inactive dogs, 18
   for Lazysagne, 165–66
   puppies relating to, 126–29

   for Slow-Cooked Chicken and Barley, 165–66
   weight relating to, 19–21, 126–29
potassium, 7, 153, 157
potato water, 32
potatoes, 31
   Beef and Potatoes, 116
   Giblet Gravy, 70
   Healthy-Kidney Potatoes and Beef, 159
Poultry Palooza, 101
Powerful Puppy Food, 131
problem behaviors
   aggression/food guarding, 184–85
   begging, 180–82
   counter surfing, 182–83
   early morning wake-up calls, 183–84
   reluctant eaters, 185–86
   speed eating, 185
prostaglandins, 138
proteins, 157, 162
   allergies relating to, 170
   amino acids from, 2–3
   as nutrient, 2–3
   L-carnitine, 153
pumpkin
   Pumpkin Ice Cream, 57
   Pumpkin Puppy Puffs, 52
   Pumpkin Puree, 71
   Pumpkin Seeds, 72
puppies
   2–3 months, 127
   4–6 months, 127
   7–9 months, 128
   10–12 months, 129
   growing, 126
   portion size relating to, 126–29
   Powerful Puppy Food, 131
   weight relating to, 126–29
Puppy Pesto, 69
Pup's Parmesan Cookies, 82

Q

quinoa
   Cluck and Quinoa Casserole, 100
   flour, 75